# CULTURE AND SYSTEM IN FAMILY THERAPY

Other titles in the

## Systemic Thinking and Practice Series

*edited by* David Campbell & Ros Draper
*published and distributed by* Karnac

Asen, E., Dawson, N., & McHugh, B. *Multiple Family Therapy: The Marlborough Model and Its Wider Applications*

Bentovim, A. *Trauma-Organized Systems. Systemic Understanding of Family Violence: Physical and Sexual Abuse*

Boscolo, L., & Bertrando, P. *Systemic Therapy with Individuals*

Burck, C., & Daniel, G. *Gender and Family Therapy*

Campbell, D., Draper, R., & Huffington, C. *Second Thoughts on the Theory and Practice of the Milan Approach to Family Therapy*

Campbell, D., Draper, R., & Huffington, C. *Teaching Systemic Thinking*

Cecchin, G., Lane, G., & Ray, W. A. *The Cybernetics of Prejudices in the Practice of Psychotherapy*

Cecchin, G., Lane, G., & Ray, W. A. *Irreverence: A Strategy for Therapists' Survival*

Dallos, R. *Interacting Stories: Narratives, Family Beliefs, and Therapy*

Draper, R., Gower, M., & Huffington, C. *Teaching Family Therapy*

Farmer, C. *Psychodrama and Systemic Therapy*

Flaskas, C., & Perlesz, A. (Eds.) *The Therapeutic Relationship in Systemic Therapy*

Fredman, G. *Death Talk: Conversations with Children and Families*

Hildebrand, J. *Bridging the Gap: A Training Module in Personal and Professional Development*

Hoffman, L. *Exchanging Voices: A Collaborative Approach to Family Therapy*

Jones, E. *Working with Adult Survivors of Child Sexual Abuse*

Jones, E., & Asen, E. *Systemic Couple Therapy and Depression*

Robinson, M. *Divorce as Family Transition: When Private Sorrow Becomes a Public Matter*

Smith, G. *Systemic Approaches to Training in Child Protection*

Wilson, J. *Child-Focused Practice: A Collaborative Systemic Approach*

**Work with Organizations**

Campbell, D. *Learning Consultation: A Systemic Framework*

Campbell, D. *The Socially Constructed Organization*

Campbell, D., Coldicott, T., & Kinsella, K. *Systemic Work with Organizations: A New Model for Managers and Change Agents*

Campbell, D., Draper, R., & Huffington, C. *A Systemic Approach to Consultation*

Cooklin, A. *Changing Organizations: Clinicians as Agents of Change*

Haslebo, G., & Nielsen, K. S. *Systems and Meaning: Consulting in Organizations*

Huffington, C., & Brunning, H. (Eds.) *Internal Consultancy in the Public Sector: Case Studies*

McCaughan, N., & Palmer, B. *Systems Thinking for Harassed Managers*

# CULTURE AND SYSTEM IN FAMILY THERAPY

*Inga-Britt Krause*

Foreword by
*Archie Smith, Jr.*

Systemic Thinking and Practice Series

Series Editors
*David Campbell & Ros Draper*

KARNAC
LONDON NEW YORK

Figure 3.1 (p. 20) reproduced by permission of Analytic Press from P. Fonagy, M. Steele, H. Steele, T. Leigh, R. Kennedy, G. Mattoon, & M. Target, "Attachment, the Reflective Self and Borderline States." In: S. Goldberg, R. Muir, & J. Kerr (Eds.), *Attachment Theory: Social, Developmental and Clinical Perspectives.* New York: Analytic Press, 1995.

First published in 2002 by
H. Karnac (Books) Ltd.
6 Pembroke Buildings, London NW10 6RE

A subsidiary of Other Press LLC, New York



**British Library Cataloguing in Publication Data**

A C.I.P. for this book is available from the British Library

ISBN: 1 85575 278 6

10 9 8 7 6 5 4 3 2 1

Edited, designed, and produced by Communication Crafts

www.karnacbooks.com

Printed & bound by Antony Rowe Ltd, Eastbourne

*To Cecilia, Farra, Marigold, Nurun, Rabia, and Raina*

# *CONTENTS*

# *ACKNOWLEDGEMENTS*

I wish to thank Farra Khan, who has worked with me with some of the clients and families about whom I write in this book. I also want to thank my clients for giving me their consent to have details about themselves recorded and referred to here. I have changed personal details as far as possible, but I am mindful that in writing about their lives I may expose them to consequences that neither I nor they can foresee. I also thank Peter Gray for his suggestions and, finally, Ros Draper and in particular David Campbell for their encouragement and comments.

# EDITORS' FOREWORD

As we acknowledge greater diversity in our society, therapists in Britain are increasingly struggling to find ways of working with clients who have different cultural backgrounds from their own. Although most of us aspire to greater cultural awareness, we frequently come up short because we lack the tools for observing culture and its affect on our own and our clients' lives. Culture, together with gender, race, sexual preference, and class, are such fundamental influences that it is difficult to step back from them to understand our own biases and the way they affect our views of clients. These influences constitute the water in the fishbowl, and we—clients and therapists—are the fish.

Britt Krause's background as an anthropologist gives her a set of tools—or, perhaps, spectacles—to help the reader know where to look to "see" culture and how to address it with clients. Many of these conceptual tools are reworkings of familiar systemic ideas. For example, she discusses meaning systems, beliefs, language, and the social construction of realities. But she also leads readers into new territory, an anthropological territory in which our behaviour, and our sense of who we are, are tightly influenced by our cultural experiences. The strength of her writing is that she forces readers to examine their own world view.

We are personally very pleased to be part of this project because Britt Krause and her ideas are increasingly influential in the family therapy community in Britain, but this is the first occasion on which she has written extensively about the application of her ideas to clinical practice. We have felt for some time that there is a great need for therapists to learn how these ideas can move from ideological debates to therapeutic conversations. And now the book has arrived! The author has explored her therapeutic interviews in detail, and her examples are diverse enough that they will be of interest to therapists who work with individuals as well as families.

*David Campbell*
*Ros Draper*
London

# *FOREWORD*

*Archie Smith, Jr.*

This is a bold and courageous book. The author meets the challenge of working across cultures and the problem of institutionalized racism head on—with courage, integrity, and intellectual strength. As an anthropologist and family therapist, Dr Britt Krause has responded to the Macpherson Report by calling for the development of competence across cultures and fundamental change within the field of systemic family practice. There are few academic and professional books within the field of family therapy that have responded to the Macpherson Report by calling for systemic awareness and fundamental change. But this book does. It demonstrates how academic ideas come together in a professional discipline and respond to a national tragedy. In this volume, Dr Krause has identified institutionalized racism as cause of a national tragedy, as an entrenched and continuing cross-cultural problem in British society. She identifies the dangers of working across cultures, but also the transforming possibilities of such work. In this way, she bridges a gap between professional competence and academic relevance. Few books in this field accomplish that. Hence, this book will be instructive for activists, students, academics, and practitioners alike.

While entrenched problems of racism and abuse of power implicate all social, political, economic, and justice institutions, Dr Krause takes care to address the institutions with which she is most familiar—mental health. She offers the field of family therapy, for example, a challenging direction when she takes the Macpherson Report as her starting point. She demonstrates systemic thinking by bringing to mind parts of a social system that may otherwise escape awareness. Dr Krause makes the connections between persons, contexts, and events that reveal the complexity of the problems, underlying patterns, and potential remedy.

Her thesis is that unquestioned and unexamined assumptions are hidden from awareness. They function as the natural standpoint of our everyday world and inform our thinking and behaviour. They shape meaning and ways of seeing. Unquestioned and unexamined assumptions play out in our interactions with others—such as colleagues and clients. They influence our beliefs of how we can (or cannot) participate in a social system. If our assumptions are unquestioned and unexamined or glossed over, then it will be difficult to critique and correct them. It will be difficult to challenge ourselves to change and grow. Systemic thinking requires the therapist to make the connections between the operation of her own assumptions in the therapeutic context and her clients. But if the therapist's own assumptions are unquestioned, unexamined, and not made a part of the system that is to be changed, then the desired therapeutic change may not be possible. When unexamined assumptions remain unquestioned, obscure, and elusive, then they contribute to the therapist's own self-deception and inability to help clients change or protect them from harm. Harm may come, unwittingly, from the practising therapist or the agency. "Professional incompetence", "collective failure", "failure of senior leadership", and/or "institutionalized racism" could be charged. Examined, as well as unexamined assumptions help to determine behaviour at the personal, collective, and institutional level. The difference that is made between examined or unexamined assumptions is enormous.

Dr Krause is calling for systemic awareness and change, including challenges to the way that we believe, practise our craft and help organize power in therapy and, by extension, in society. This leads me to address a fundamental message in Dr Krause's book, namely belief as one of several systemic ideas.

Beliefs are of many different types and may range from secular to religious, simple to complex, rational to irrational and non-rational, individual and collective, and so on. Beliefs are important. They form maps in the mind which arise from our experiences. They help to shape our assumptive world. They influence our emotions, perceptions, actions, and relations.

In a general way, beliefs may be thought of as soft and hard. Soft beliefs are opinions. An opinion is a belief or conclusion held with confidence but not substantiated by proof. In some instances, an opinion may reflect prevailing social view. Opinions are important and help us to manage our day-to-day living, but they may also be relatively easy to change or may be discarded when they no longer serve our purposes. To change opinions may not cause us a great deal of stress, because they are not an integral part of our world view. Hard beliefs are of a very different nature. They are hard-won convictions. They are about the way things are. Hard beliefs or convictions are not easily changed because they have been internalized and take longer to develop or sediment. Convictions form the bedrock of our assumptive world and operate outside our awareness. Therefore, they are not readily available for serious challenge nor are they easy to change even when disconfirming evidence is presented.

Therapists are interested in all sorts of beliefs and are especially interested in the distinction between soft and hard beliefs. How, then, can convictions or hard beliefs be addressed and changed? If our assumptions are hidden and unquestioned, then how can we know them? How can we find out? We must ask, argues Dr Krause. But how can we ask if we do not know? How can we find out if we do not ask? These are among some of the thorny questions that Dr Krause addresses in the light of the Macpherson Report and in the context of doing therapy across cultural differentness.

By utilizing the Macpherson Report as her starting point, Dr Krause alerts us to the important distinction between mere opinions and convictions. The indifference and collective failure that underlay the police investigation into the Stephen Lawrence murder had a long history with roots in social convention, unquestioned assumptions, and institutionalized practices which function in everyday life as business-as-usual. This phenomenon of indifference and collective failure is not limited to the police. It is a feature of so-called democratic institutions. As a systemic thinker, Britt Krause draws upon this report and makes connections to her disciplines of anthropology and family therapy. She raises certain fundamental and ethnographic questions that would enable us to move beyond the level of opinion to question the convictions that are embodied in our practices and embedded in our unexamined assumptions and theories. She adapts Barbara Herrnstein Smith's "language loops" and gives us tools to develop cultural competence. These tools include the culture and context of therapy, culture as a system, and social systems that maintain as well as transmit value consensus, meaning, and behaviour. Systemic thinking and cultural competence are developed by giving us tools to work at the collective level while holding in mind "the relevant systems", patterns, structures, social relations, and differences between persons. In this way, the competence of the therapist is enabled when helping people change the beliefs and patterns that contribute to suffering and trauma in their lives and in the lives of others.

I welcome this book from Dr Britt Krause, who brings her ethnographic insights as an anthropologist and her training and practice as a systemic family therapist. Here she builds upon her previous work, *Therapy across Culture*. In so doing she sounds the alarm that therapy cannot be conducted as business-as-usual in a society in which failure to protect the basic, ostensibly inalienable rights of culturally different citizens (or strangers) is a daily occurrence.

# CULTURE AND SYSTEM IN FAMILY THERAPY

*CHAPTER ONE*

# Introduction

In 1998, a significant event took place in race relations in Britain. This was the Stephen Lawrence Inquiry. Stephen Lawrence was murdered by a small gang of young white men as he waited for a bus. His murder was not properly investigated, and to date no one has been found guilty of it. However, the public inquiry that eventually took place found the Metropolitan Police guilty of negligence and institutional racism, and in the weeks that followed the publication of the report on the inquiry (Macpherson, 1999), radio and television news, newspaper editorials, and commentaries as well as private conversations were focused on these events and their implications. Many people, including young Afro-Caribbean, Asian, and white British, attended the inquiry, and a play—*The Colour of Justice*—based on verbatim transcripts of the inquiry was screened on television at peak viewing time. The inquiry into the murder of Stephen Lawrence openly placed an obligation on the Establishment to address issues of racism and discrimination in a different way from what had previously been done. This was no easy matter, and although there have since been important and essential initiatives—such as the introduction of the

Race Relations (Amendment) Act into the public sector during 2000—it is perhaps too early to say whether the implications of the Macpherson Report have been recognized by the public, the government, and professionals in key public services in Britain. These implication are indeed far-reaching and therefore difficult to face.

The difficulty is to be found in the notion of institutionalized racism to which the report drew attention. Lord Justice Macpherson and his team defined institutionalized racism as

> The collective failure of an organisation to provide an appropriate and professional service to people because of their colour, culture and ethnic origin. It can be seen or detected in processes, attitudes and behaviour which amount to discrimination through unwitting prejudice, ignorance, thoughtlessness and racist stereotyping which disadvantage minority ethnic people. [Macpherson, 1999, p. 28]

Why is this difficult?

The key words in the definition are "collective failure", "unwitting prejudice", "ignorance", and "thoughtlessness". These are notions that suggest that a person may not quite know what he or she is doing and that addressing these areas is more complicated than simply saying "I won't do it again" or "If only we can find persons who are not at fault in this way". Taking this view of race relations in Britain was a step forward from a previous report, *The Brixton Disorders*, produced by Lord Scarman after the uprisings in several English cities in 1981 (Scarman, 1981). This earlier report had acknowledged that some police officers were racially prejudiced, but it had also suggested that this was an occasional occurrence in a few instances and that it was irrational.

The period between 1981 and 1993, the year of Stephen Lawrence's murder, was characterized by an impasse in race relations. The identification and removal of individual persons known to be racist in the police and in other institutions did not change the situation much. In some ways, this approach actually helped maintain the racist status quo by obscuring the real issues. Why? Because racism and discrimination cannot be explained solely by referring to mechanisms residing inside individuals (Henriques, 1984). They are also produced in the processes and interactions that make up social relationships. They are collective rather than individual, and, being collective, they are not always fully within the awareness of persons. Macpherson's focus on collective failures and unwitting prejudice acknowledged this and was a step from the individual to the relational or socially constructed point of view. However, this shift also challenges the Establishment and our institutions in several different ways and is difficult to pursue as a public debate.

I have drawn attention to these events firstly because they are relevant to psychotherapy and secondly because they set the frame for the questions that I want to address in this book. These are questions that must be addressed specifically when working with families cross-culturally in therapy, but they also are relevant to intracultural work. The Stephen Lawrence Inquiry and the Macpherson Report remind us that it is not only in the therapy-room that intimate aspects of awareness, accommodation, and understanding take place. These are also political concerns and questions of human rights. These different spheres are not disconnected. Public and private domains are not separate, because values and attitudes are reproduced and shaped in both (Geertz, 1998). Racist murders and the public response to such events are also relevant to psychotherapists, because as citizens and participants in social processes in Britain, psychotherapists are no different from other persons who, whatever their culture, ethnicity, or skin colour, are touched and implicated in some way in these processes. Collective failures implicate everyone, although those who start out from a privileged position are implicated in a different way from those who do not.

Where, then, in systemic or family psychotherapy do we find the "collective failures" mentioned in the Macpherson Report? This is one of the questions that I address in this book. The general answer is that we find them in our assumptions—that is to say, in our public and personal values and norms. More specifically, we find them in the way our organizations work and in our ideas about gender, about the family, and about kinship and social relationships. We also find them in our professional theories and concepts, which sometimes—supported by histories of scientific developments, trials of clinical practice, a "fit" with prevailing ideology, and a particular arrangement of relations of power—take on such status of "truth" that they become part of the way that things, naturally, are for us.

This is above all when failure sets in: when our theories and conventions prevent us from recognizing that they may not be universally shared and when we fail to keep in mind that some of the things we ourselves do, and the ways we feel or think, are also socially constructed.

This book aims to help the psychotherapist who works with clients who are culturally and ethnically different from herself to address these difficult issues and find an anti-discriminatory, non-ethnocentric, and ethical way of working cross-culturally.* I do not suggest that therapists or anyone else annul their own assumptions. To my mind this would be impossible and would produce thoughts and actions without coherence and of no use. Rather, I shall suggest how we can use our knowledge about our own assumptions to ask appropriate and curious questions and, in this way, with our clients enter a common space for communicating. Entering this space entails that as far as is possible we try to see things from our clients' point of view, and this means aiming to understand them against the background of the contexts in which they live. I think that this must be a necessary condition for ethical and non-discriminatory cross-cultural therapy.

Contexts are, of course, physical and local. This means that they are social (economic, political, familial) and cultural, and this is why I here consider as I have elsewhere (Krause, 1998), that cross-cultural therapy requires a systemic approach. As I see it, the strength of systemic psychotherapy is the importance placed in this approach on relationships between parts, individuals or events rather than on these entities in themselves. This is a characteristic of all systemic psychotherapy approaches, whether first-order, second-order, strategic, or constructionist/narrative, and this accords well with sociological or social anthropological approaches. Societies, nations, or groups of people are made up of embodied individuals in multiple overlapping relationships (Giddens, 1984; Ingold, 1986; Jenkins, 1997) in which meanings are expressed, reconstituted, or changed over time (Bateson, 1973; Taylor, 1985). It is

*In general discussions, feminine pronouns are used for therapists and carers, and masculine pronouns for infants.

impossible to have a theory about society which makes propositions only about individuals and not about their interaction and communication. But it is also the case that in all societies the idea of *relationships* and *relating* is valued, even though, as in England, America, and parts of Europe today, this may be articulated negatively. The idea of relationships captures a universal human predicament, even when in some societies this idea is framed and expressed in unique cultural and local terms. For these reasons, I consider that therapeutic approaches that aim to address social and cultural issues (and none can avoid this altogether) must also incorporate a systems view in some way.

In this respect, I do not want to draw a distinction between family therapy and systemic psychotherapy. To me, family therapy is an earlier name for an approach that focuses on relationships. This name tells us something about how the approach came about historically, and, although the approach has since been developed and improved by its practitioners becoming interested in wider systems and in culture, something fundamental remains to be recognized about "first relationships". The "family" is a cross-cultural idea even though the processes, functions, shapes, terms, and structures that are associated with this idea are not. The same is not quite the case for "system". "System" is more of an abstraction. That is to say, "systems" are everywhere but may not be recognized and named, and there is much less cross-cultural agreement. This does not mean that the idea of "system" cannot be useful, but that "system" as well as "family" are examples of the care and thought needed in order to avoid institutionalized discrimination. I do not therefore see my own approach as being in one camp rather than another, and I use the terms "systemic psychotherapy" and "family therapy" interchangeably to refer broadly to this field. I shall, however, discuss the different emphases that different approaches bring forth, and even though I consider that any systemic approach has a head start over individual ones, in the chapters to come I shall also show that systemic approaches are not necessarily culture-free. In fact, in a general sense nothing is culture-free, and this is why an emphasis on culture may provide a profoundly critical evaluation of what we do as therapists.

In this book, then, I suggest ways of thinking and theorizing about this, and I also suggest practical steps that can be taken to ensure that such a critique is carried out in a responsible and disciplined way. Part I offers a theoretical overview of how modern and postmodern approaches may be integrated; part II examines some of my own cross-cultural clinical material. Finally, the Appendix outlines a model—which, following Barbara Herrnstein Smith, I call "a reflective loop"—that can be used in the beginning stages of therapy and in training and also at any point when therapists feel that the cross-cultural validity of their work may be in question. In the spirit of Macpherson, I shall urge that cultural questioning and self-reflection become integral to the ongoing practice and theorizing in family therapy. I think that only in this way will therapists be able to claim that they try to avoid practices that are institutionally discriminating and unjust.

*PART I*

# CULTURE AND SYSTEMIC THINKING

CHAPTER TWO

# System

The transition from modern to postmodern practices in family therapy has been described in different ways—first-order/second order, objective/constructionist, systemic/narrative (Anderson, 1999; Bertrando, 2000; Combs & Freedman, 1998; Dallos, 1997; Dallos & Urry, 1999; Falicov, 1998; Gower, 1999; Hoffman, 1998; Minuchin, 1998, 1999; Pocock, 1995, 1999; Weingarten, 1998). Another way of describing this is to say that there has been a shift in the use of the idea of "the system". Early systemic ideas were influenced by cybernetics as applied to mechanical systems: steam engines, pistons, and central-heating systems, and so on (Watzlawick, Beavin, & Jackson, 1967). In contrast, in postmodern thinking about systems in family therapy, a system is unmistakably a social system. Of course, social bonds between people have been considered before. Family therapists such as Murray Bowen, Salvador Minuchin, and the early Milan team based much of their practice on the emotional connectedness between family members and in this way implicitly acknowledged the influence of social systems. Gregory Bateson too had a social system in mind when he applied cybernetics to the Iatmul Naven ritual (Bateson,

1958). His analysis of this ritual was a milestone in the attempt to incorporate the two models into a theory about human communication which could unite physical and social phenomena (Bateson, 1973, 1979). The important synthesis of Bateson's work was not, however, fully recognized at that time, and when Paul Watzlawick published *Pragmatics of Human Communication* (Watzlawick et al., 1967), a classic family therapy text, Bateson was hurt and angered that his close colleague should independently have published work that did not, in as far as it considered communication in isolation from cultural communication, adequately reflect the complexity of the issues on which they had both been working together (Harries-Jones, 1995, p. 28).

Other points of difference emerge from these two different ways of conceptualizing a system. Mechanical systems operate according to rules or forces that are assumed to operate in the same way anywhere and at any time if the external conditions are the same. This is pretty much the case, for example, with a central-heating circuit. When Bateson worked with the Iatmul, this was also the way anthropologists understood the working of societies: as patterns that could be discovered (Krause, 1998). What above all was to be discovered was whether cross-cultural patterns could be identified everywhere and to what extent regional social differences and similarities existed and (within a more hidden agenda) how "we" could make sense of "them". Anthropologists are now less likely to write about patterns or about "structure" and "organization", but for Bateson a social system consisted of patterns of emotions, cognitions, and behaviours (Bateson, 1958). In the context of anthropology, this emphasis on "relationship" or relationality has always been important (Ingold, 1986; Krause, 1994) and is receiving new scrutiny (Strathern, 1999). In the context of psychiatry, it was this insight that provided the possibility of a radical shift from a focus on the patient to a focus on the patient-in-relationships central to systemic approaches in family therapy.

In contrast, postmodern approaches to family therapy are not explicitly concerned with rules and patterns. The emphasis tends to be on individual variation and on the uniqueness of individual stories, and this uniqueness is seen to be derived from the complex interaction of persons in social systems and from the way individual persons access ideologies such as beliefs and language in particular ways. From this point of view, the world is a place where patterns or systematic processes are themselves bundles of variation, and accordingly observation or research are aimed at the effects of the destabilization of patterns (Gergen, 1994, p. 135). Constructionist and narrative approaches in family therapy therefore tend to place less emphasis on repetition, routinization, and regularity and more on variation and multiplicity.

This description is, of course, a bit of a caricature. Constructionists do not dissociate themselves completely from systemic thinking. Indeed, this would be impossible. The emphasis on individual variation is possible *because* it is variation *from* a pattern, and the constructionist makes a choice about what to concentrate on. The constructionist emphasis on the individual-in-social contexts, albeit at the expense of the collectivity, therefore *is* an emphasis on social relationships, and implicitly it is based on some notion of a social system. When Minuchin recently complained that postmodern family therapists are no longer concerned with the family, he appeared to be commenting on what he saw narrative family therapists do and not on how narrative family therapists think about what they do (Minuchin, 1998). But if we consider both levels of activity, it is clear that the idea of "a system" has not disappeared; rather, it has gone out of focus. One could say, therefore, that because postmodern approaches in some way have developed from modern ones, the idea of system has become an assumption to which it is no longer necessary to refer or to theorize directly about.

I believe that this is unhelpful because assumptions easily become hidden as "the way things naturally are" and are difficult to critique. I also believe that to leave "system" as an idea that is unexamined from a cross-cultural point of view may be or may become a collective failure in family therapy (Macpherson, 1999). In this book I therefore want to bring the idea of "the system" back into the foreground of thinking in family therapy and I want to suggest that in cross-cultural work such a re-examination is crucial. This is because culture itself is a systemic idea. I begin by showing how "system" has become a hidden assumption of narrative approaches in family therapy.

## *System and constructionism in family therapy*

Constructionist or narrative therapy are general labels that categorize several different styles and approaches together. So, for example, experience may be accessed in a number of different ways: it can be accessed narrowly through a scrutiny of language and text using discourse analysis (Burck, Frosh, Strickland-Clark, & Morgan, 1998; Frosh, Burck, Strickland-Clark, & Morgan, 1996) or more widely by paying attention to discourse defined to include thoughts and ideas manifested in language and to the way social practices reproduce and coincide with themes of meaning in a given context (Bruner, 1990; Foucault, 1973, 1979; Gergen, 1994; White, 1992). It is perhaps this latter version that is most often identified with the label narrative/constructionist in systemic psychotherapy, and with it has also followed the notion that other aspects of the traditional systemic approaches—such as the therapist as expert and of the therapist as being outside the system and in some way "objective"—should be rejected (Andersen, 1991, 1992; Anderson & Goolishian, 1988, 1992).

Everyone can agree that what happens in therapy depends quite a lot on what the therapist does and what she does not do. Whether the therapist is a "master conversationalist" (Anderson & Goolishian, 1988) or "a friendly editor" (Hoffman in Simon, 1992; Hoffman, 1993) or "a liberator of subjugated knowledges and life stories" (White & Epston, 1990)—and these different stances do not have similar implications—she must interact and communicate with her clients. Here lies the rub, because in this interaction the therapist must use some ideas about what she is doing and about what she is going to do, and she is usually more aware of some of these ideas than she is about others. This is because the ideas and "guidelines" and the theory that the therapist uses are derived from her own participation in a social system in which certain meanings and discourses prevail. She must use her own notions about relationships over time and about how the world is organized and systematized, and this social knowledge derives from the social context and the ideology, both personal and professional, in which the therapist herself has grown up and has been trained. This means that, by virtue of her own participation in a society and in a culture, the therapist herself has some notion of a system of relationships and meanings, some social knowledge. Let me illustrate what I am getting at with an example from a recent article discussing the therapy style of Michael White, a well-known and accomplished social constructionist/narrative therapist.

In this article, Kogan and Gale (1997), themselves systemic psychotherapists, examined the text of a therapy session conducted by Michael White, a white, male, heterosexual therapist, in order to study the way White manages therapeutic conversations. White gave a consultation to a couple and their therapist on stage in a conference, and Kogan and Gale presented verbatim excerpts from this in their article. The excerpts were transcribed according to conventions in conversational analysis—that is to say, giving the reader information about lengths of pauses, emphasis, repetitions, and so forth. The reader was also told that the couple were white and heterosexual, and their ages were given; some minimal information was presented regarding the background to their coming to therapy. The analysis proceeded well within the confines of the text, showing White's considerable skill in decentring himself and in developing reciprocity and mutuality between himself and his clients through micro-shifts in the use of key words, repetitions, and shifts of emphasis. In the article, the excerpts continued more or less without a clarifying commentary until such a time when the woman in the couple mentioned "control" and "her having to be in control" (Kogan & Gale, 1997, p. 114). At this point, Kogan and Gale offered a cultural commentary. They wrote:

> Culturally, the word "control" is especially loaded for females in the family context; they face the double bind of being assumed to have responsibility for family relationships, and yet they must not appear to be in a position of running things (Bograd, 1988). "Controlling" as applied to females, is typically negative and associated with the culture's discomfort with female power. [p. 115]

This was the first time the authors interrupted their discussion of the flow of the therapy with a reference to another source, namely Bograd's paper. At this point, they were no longer simply drawing on their own experience of the therapy conducted by White or relying on their own resources. The gender issue appeared to call for additional emphasis, namely a professional reference cast in "scientific language" (i.e. using the term "females" rather than "women").

In their article the effect of this reference was to establish the legitimacy of a particular ideology relating to gender relations in Anglo-American societies. Since the couple were white, heterosexual, and Anglo-American, this did not pose any problems. In fact, most of us would probably agree that White, and Kogan and Gale, were on to an important issue for this couple and that the conversation and the commentary were culturally sensitive. However, this should not prevent us from thinking about what is going on. I think that when Kogan and Gale diverted from the text of the therapy session in order to interpret and explicate a cultural theme, namely "control", they were drawing on their own—and in this case generally accepted—professional knowledge about relations between men and women in their own society. I am not suggesting that they were wholly conscious of what they were doing or that they were in any way dishonest (Bertrando, 2000). I am suggesting that the knowledge they used is socially constituted—that is to say, it has some coherence because it is shared and changed through social relationships. In this way, Kogan and Gale referred to and used, as did White, an idea of a system which they have gained from their participation in their own social systems.

This idea of a system is contained in the connection that they made between a general notion of gender relationships and the words and sentiments communicated by the couple during the consultation. In this they (rightly) took for granted a connection between individual dispositions, interactions, and relationships between persons and ideas about the right (in the sense of generally accepted) way of doing things (Jenkins, 1997). Indeed, readers need to receive a minimum of interpretation because Michael White, the couple, their original therapist, and Kogan and Gale—and probably the typical readership of the influential journal in which the article appeared—all understand, have access to, and operate more or less similar background information about the way social (gender) relationships operate in Anglo-American societies. Therefore familiarity with basic premises can reasonably be assumed, and similar or overlapping interpretations can be expected. The reader need receive only a minimum of contextualizing and descriptive commentary and the rest is more or less obvious. But this should not blind us to the fact that interpretation is taking place and that White and Kogan and Gale are using premises and themes derived outside the therapy context and acquired before the consultation or the writing of the article. The participants do not come to this "cold". They have each built on their own experiences of relationships over time—that is to say, on their own experiences of social systems and with their own versions of social knowledge.

This must be so, since each of us has been brought up and matured in a context of particular social relationships and particular social meanings. But this is also *the* challenge: to notice when we move from what belongs to others to what belongs to ourselves. In the case of Kogan and Gale's article, this was marked by the change of material: from the communication between the couple and the therapists in the consultation to a reference to a scientific study. I cannot be sure about the validity of the scientific study for the couple, and without checking the reference I must take the authors' word for it. And yet even with this caveat the scientific reference is useful, not as a testimony of the way things are with the couple (because I cannot know this till I check it out) but as evidence of the authors' own train of thought and assumptions. For them, and for me, the reference, which occurs to them as relevant, offers an opportunity for checking the idea about "control". It would be the same if the reference did not exist and the idea about gender and control occurred to them because it reminded them about their own lives, or about a novel they had read or a film they had watched. All these contexts may provide good ideas, but for these to be valid or shown to be valid in a particular case they need checking out. It is thus not so much a question of observation or (as in my case right now) observation of observation as a detached activity, but of thinking about, grasping, feeling, or getting in touch with observation as a kind of participation that activates a particular view.

I suggest therefore that in this case (as well as in all cases) the therapists are using (as all therapists must) a model of a system. This system is a social system in which persons are connected to other persons, and they all in turn are connected to ideas about the way things should be done. In this way, clients and therapists all have some notions of a social system and their own participation in it. What varies is the extent to which the idea that the therapists have and the idea that the clients have overlap or are congruent. The social knowledge of therapists is a combination of personal experience, education, and professional training; however, as mental health professionals, therapists have particular responsibilities in their use of social knowledge. This is because of their role in the creation and continuation of particular discourses, ideologies, and institutions of deficit and pathology (Gergen, 1994). The meeting in the therapy-room or in the consultation is thus different from a meeting outside this professional context, and this is the reason why therapists carry particular responsibilities to understand what they are doing. Although clients, too, participate, they do not of course carry quite the same responsibility.

I have, then, so far suggested that in all family therapy approaches there are more or less explicit assumptions about a "system" and that what is different in the different approaches is the emphasis that this collectivity receives and the extent to which it is theorized. What, then, of culture in these approaches? Because meaning can only be constituted, changed, and continued in social relationships and interaction, the terms "social system" and "culture" and the phenomena to which they refer implicate each other. The narrative/constructionist emphasis on developing an understanding of clients' world view, on co-construction in the therapeutic process, and on deconstructing meaning shows an awareness that discourse is culturally constructed. Does this mean that the narrative/constructionist approach ensures sensitive and ethical cross-cultural practice? Would White's technique have been different had the couple been Bangladeshi or Somali, for example? What is at issue here is not only the extent to which therapists can acknowledge cultural and ideological differences, but also the nature and role of theory. Before I turn to these questions, we need to take a closer look at culture.

CHAPTER THREE

# Culture

"Culture" is notoriously difficult to define (Carrithers, 1992; Ingold, 1986; Krause, 1998; Kuper, 1999; Nuckolls, 1998), part of the difficulty being that culture is both inside and outside persons. By that I do not mean that culture is something inherently intrinsic to individual persons—that would be a contradiction in terms. I mean that culture is internalized in individuals insofar as a person's thoughts, feelings, intentions, and motivations are constructed according to and with the influence of cultural conventions. This means that when persons think and feel, they always do so through culture; however, some cultural conventions, although different, may have similar orientations, and when we communicate with people whose cultural backgrounds are more or less the same as our own, culture may virtually disappear from view. Ethnographers, anthropologists, and family therapists therefore never observe culturally unmediated sequences of interaction and communication, nor does any one else for that matter. We cannot access facts, although some conditions may implicate value less than others. For example, the treatment of a broken leg may require less cross-cultural knowledge than a case of spirit possession, but both conditions implicate cultural knowledge because treatment of persons requires communication. A broken leg may, for example, be considered as a misfortune due to witchcraft or sorcery or bad luck or as a result of a fall or an accident. Each of these explanations is cultural, even though you may want to argue (which in this instance I do not) that some are more adequate, true, or rational than others.

The existence of cultural differences raises the question of relativism. Extreme cultural relativism is absurd, for this would mean that no cross-cultural communication can be possible, which is manifestly not the case. Of course, power and inequality in terms of access to wealth and knowledge affect cross-cultural communication, but this is a different matter. Two people from different cultures, even if they speak different languages, can have some kind of conversation with each other. Weaker forms of relativism are much more difficulty to dispute, and the question of how far and how deeply cultural differences run is one that has been at the centre of much philosophical debate. It is also one that is curiously sensitive and tends to raise tempers and lodge debaters into polarized camps. Constructionists favour the view that meanings and language are dependent on social usage—that is to say, on the way people use ideas and words in their immediate, day-to-day communication with each other. Because this emphasizes variation and multiplicity, constructionism is a form of relativism. While modern scientific approaches consider variation a supreme methodological difficulty, constructionism considers this to be a basic premise from which everything else follows.

Culture is also about differences and variation, but cultural differences and orientations clearly persist with some (not complete) continuity over time, so how can therapists navigate through this without being pulled to either universalist or relativist extremes? What assumptions can we reasonably make about where culture is located? I say reasonably here because I am not concerned with scientific "truth" but, rather, with which point of view may provide useful insight. Professionals orientated towards science and modernity prefer to claim that "scientific" discoveries—such as schizophrenia, depression, and Alzheimer's disease—are valid in all cultures, whereas other professionals, including postmodern constructionists, may consider that questions of cross-cultural validity are largely irrelevant. Recent attachment-theory research has suggested a model for interpersonal relationships which goes some way towards mediating these two opposed positions, and this will serve as a useful point of departure for my project here regarding the location of culture and how therapists might proceed in cross-cultural work.

I want to refer to a paper written by Fonagy and his colleagues (Fonagy et al., 1995) in which they discuss the predictive value of the Adult Attachment Interview for pathological emotional development. I am not concerned with the full extent of their material here. What is of interest to me, and I suggest also to therapists who practise cross-culturally, is the model of the mother–infant relationship which this team uses. Attachment research has for many years used an object-relations model to understand carer–infant interaction and communication, and from this model, together with many observations of (mostly) middle-class American mother–infant pairs, several standardized interviews have been developed. One is the Adult Attachment Interview (Main & Goldwyn, 1984, 1985/1991). This is a standardized interview of an adult carer through which something can be learned about the way this adult represents her own intimate social relationships. The interview also illuminates the way this representation affects the attachment between this carer and her child and her child's attachment to her. This material is interesting for my purpose here because it aims to access not only the way the world looks to an individual, be it mother or child, but also the way that the outlook of one of them—that is, the mother—affects the way the world is experienced by the child. It is a reflexive enquiry, and, for questions about how culture is passed on, this is clearly a useful place to start.

The traditional model suggested by Bowlby (1969) assumed that when a child grows up she will use an internalized image or notion of his carer (most often referred to as mother), and if this caregiver herself is capable of emotional containment, this will help the child control conflict and distress (Figure 3.1a). A child is therefore successfully socialized when he has been able to convert his carer to an internal image of caring and containment. The revised model suggested by Fonagy and his colleagues changes the

A

B

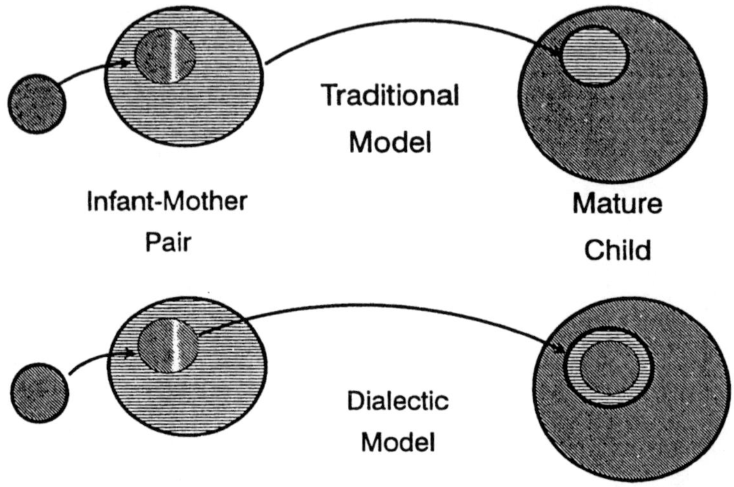


FIGURE 3.1: The traditional model of attachment assumes that the caregiver is internalized and in this way provides internal control of affect. The dialectic model assumes that it is the caregiver's image of the intentional infant which becomes internalized and henceforth constitutes the core of the child's mentalizing self. (From Fonagy et al., 1995.)

emphasis in the model from experience of behaviour to the experience of reflection (Figure 3.1b). In this model, not only does the child internalize an image of his carer's stance, but within this image is also included the carer's stance towards the child as a thinking, believing, and desiring human being. In other words, the child does not only internalize an image of his carer, but with this image comes an image of himself comprehended though his carer's stance to him, and it is this composite image that becomes the child's self. It is not, then, simply a question of an image but, rather, of a process.

> The child not only perceives in the caregiver's behaviour her mentalising stance, which he has to assume in order to account for her behaviour, but, in particular, perceives the caregiver's stance vis-à-vis an image of him as mentalizing, desiring and believing. This representation is internalized. If the caregiver's reflective capacity enables her accurately to picture the infant's intentional stance, the infant has the opportunity to "find himself in the other" as a mentalizing individual. [Fonagy et al., 1995, p. 257]

The process is a mental process, which begins for the child in earnest at the moment of the first carer–infant interaction. As far as the carer is concerned, for her this process also began at the first moment of interaction with her own first carers. Both infant and carer are considered to be influenced by others through interactive and mutual relationships in which others reflect about them and they in turn reflect about others.

This revised model is, of course, an excellent example of what is meant by social construction: the child's self and his emotional orientation to other persons is a result of ongoing, reflexive social relationships that begin at or before birth and continue till death. As we are talking about thinking, feeling, and believing as well as about acting, we are also talking about cultural themes, which through micro-processes give meaning to relationships, both those that can be observed through interaction and those that, as the model suggests, are internalized mental images and processes. Accordingly, culture is implicated not only in selfhood, but also in models of the mind, in relationships, in emotion, in attachment, and in ideas about child care. Culture is not only what can be heard and seen, such as dress, behaviour, etiquette, art, artefacts, language, and music. Culture is also implicated in what lies behind these, such as orientation, emotion, intention, motivation, ideas, and memories, and these cannot easily be observed. Culture is deeply embedded in social relationships and, like language, offers to persons a repertoire of behaviour and meaning. In terms of its effect on individual persons, culture cannot, then, be seen to be the icing on the cake, nor can it be described as a layer cake or even a marble cake. If we want to use this sort of analogy of the relationship between the individual and cultural processes, we must say that "culture cooks the cake" (Strawson, 1996). The ingredients—or, in the case of persons, the capacity—may be seen as universal, but the amalgamation or the presentation—the cake or the person, as the case may be—is relative. This does not, however, mean that we do not from time to time get a glimpse of the raw material or the human condition. That is to say, to hold this view does not altogether exclude some kind of universalism. This is a matter to which I return later.

### *Culture is a kind of system?*

The revised attachment model is persuasive because it points to the complexity of interactive and social processes and, in particular, because it points to the reciprocity between infants and carers both in the way they interact and think about each other and also in the way they anticipate each other's responses. This can be observed and experienced in everyday life, not only between infants and their carers but also between persons in any social interaction. Think, for example, of playing a game. The players in a football team must not only be ready to respond when the ball is kicked to them, but must also anticipate this by moving into the right position and being ready to receive the ball. It is the same with any other coordinated action involving two or more people: driving a car in traffic, playing music together, dancing, or a conversation are a few examples. Agents respond and expect to respond to the actions of other agents, and they also expect that others will do the same. The responses must be more or less satisfactory or effective for all parties (Smith, 1997) or else the game or the interaction will not continue. Persons will part, players will stop playing the game, the conversation will finish. And these interactions and responses do not only take place through an exchange of words. The football players or the motorists may shout to or at each other, but equally often the communications to which others respond are not verbal but a bodily cue, a movement, or an indication. The infant also does not use words, even though his carer—especially in Anglo-American cultures—may place particular value on teaching him verbal skills. The model thus reminds us that in our thinking about this we should not take meaning to be confined to words but, rather, that language must be seen to include the full range of responsive human actions. There cannot be any action or object perceived by me or any other person without meaning, and this is of course the well known point made by Hoffman (1993) that persons see the world through cultural lenses. Culture always implicates meaning, and the new-born infant is not only surrounded by meaning and culture, but is also rapidly internalizing these phenomena through the vehicle of the reflexive sequences of interaction and communication with his carers.

The carer, then, has a crucial job to do, and this is of course one of the points emphasized by attachment theory. I turn to this now not because I am concerned to discuss adequate and inadequate parenting, although this is a concern for cross-cultural therapeutic practice, but because the position of the carer in the model demonstrates how important it is that we do not lose sight of notions of "time", "pattern", and "system" in thinking about culture. What goes for the infant in the revised attachment model must also go for the carer when she was an infant. That is to say, the carer too internalized her own caregiver's notion of her as a desiring, believing, or mentalizing being, and this came to constitute an important part of her self and her experience of it. She also learnt about herself and about how she may respond to others through the way her carer responded to her responding to her carer. The same could, of course, be said for the caregiver's carer and his or her carer, and so forth. No individual can exist before the social relationships that connects him or her to other persons in this chain or in any other part of social life. It is only through the interaction and communication with persons in relationships that infants acquire knowledge about what to do and what not to do both vis-à-vis their carers and vis-à-vis any other persons with whom they come into contact. This is because carers do not only communicate their own views based on their own private experiences to their infants, they also communicate their relationships, ideas and attitudes towards other persons with whom they, the carers, have continuing relationships. So, for example, if a mother is very much loved by her brother and this uncle also adores his niece, meets with her often and gives gifts regularly, this will sooner or later become an aspect that influences the child's idea of familial relationships. Now, if the mother lives in a society in which particular value is placed on the relationship between herself and her brother—they may perhaps have rights in each other's persons (bodily substances or property)—and by extension between her brother and her daughter, so that it would be a mother's expectations even before she has children that her brother will be closely involved in the upbringing of his niece, this would then have further and perhaps different effects on the child's orientation to family life, on her dreams, and on her motivations and intentions. I have taken this example because such a case has in fact been argued by some anthropologists in response to the debate about the universality of the Oedipus complex (Krause, 1998; Kurtz, 1992; Obeyesekere, 1990). However, the general point is this: that carers themselves are social agents involved in many social relationships, so that as well as responding to their children as responsive and mentalizing agents, carers also communicate to their children their responses to other responsive and mentalizing agents with whom they are involved. Infants and children therefore do not only learn a language as a catalogue of words; they also learn a language including material bodies, experiential histories, and ongoing social interactions. We can say that what infants learn is a kind of cultural system, a collection of norms and values that have some continuity over time, and, of course, integral to this is meaning. Over time there is, then, some continuity in what persons experience, in what they do, in what they think, and in the concepts and words they use. Such continuities Bateson (1973) called patterns, and, as my example of the sister/brother/niece above suggests, in more complex sequences of meanings and interactions different patterns are connected, so that with pattern we must also talk about system. If culture then implies patterns in the sense of continuity of meaning over time, what kind of system is a cultural or a social system?

CHAPTER FOUR

# Culture and system

## System again

We have come a long way away from the model of a mechanical system mentioned in chapter two, in which different elements or parts are tightly interconnected and the relationship between them is a causal one, so that whenever something happens to one element this always has the same, predictable effect on other elements. Although this mechanical idea of a system has been used by both anthropologists and family therapists, it is a caricature of the processes that take place in social systems, and there are at least three reasons for this.

### *Boundaries*

First, it is impossible to delineate the boundaries of a social system in the way that this can be done for a mechanical one. A social system is a collectivity of persons who are connected indirectly or directly though ongoing social relationships and who more or less agree on the use of certain cultural conventions, words, signs, themes of meaning. It can perhaps be characterized as a community and associated with a locality, but this does not fit straightforwardly with the experience of the increasing numbers of displaced persons or diasporas (Brah, 1996). Much more important for a social system is that in considering themselves members, persons take part (sometimes only momentarily) in processes that distinguish them from members of other social systems, groups, or communities (Banks, 1996; Barth, 1969; Jenkins, 1997). A social system is therefore characterized by social processes that differentiate members of it from members of other social systems and not so much by the criteria of membership, be these signs, symbols, ancestry, or locality, even though each of these may be the focus for highlighting the differences. Social systems, then, can only be defined roughly.

### *"More-or-less" patterns*

Second, because the agents in social systems are persons, and because social systems involve a large number of persons, no reliable predictions can be made about how a change in one pattern will affect other patterns. Cultural and social patterns are therefore "more-or-less patterns". To explain this, we may examine what is involved in a conversation or an interaction. In this, I follow Barbara Herrnstein Smith (1997) and what she has referred to as "the language loop" (pp. 52–72), an idea that she does not confine to words or linguistic theory. "The language loop" goes something like this: persons from the same community tend to produce more or less the same actions, either verbal or non-verbal, as a response to a range of circumstances in their lives. That is to say, there is a limit to the variation that one would find if the reactions of all members of a community were studied. Other persons from the same community also tend to react to these actions in ways that the first group of persons consider more or less appropriate. Because these actions and reactions have taken place regularly before, and because persons therefore know that others will react to particular circumstances including their own communications in more or less expected ways, persons learn that by producing certain communications they can affect the feelings and sentiments and therefore the behaviour of others who are listening or receiving these communications. This kind of reciprocal impact will continue as long as the messages or communications continue to evoke a reaction from all parties.

If you prefer the football-game analogy, it goes something like this. The players on the football team may say that they are only successful when they win a match. But they may also recognize that a particular game has been effective when they have played well as a team. Good teamwork means that members are able to respond well to each other and that each pass of the ball by one player is good enough to enable another player to receive it and pass it on effectively. It may also encompass the making of mistakes—that is, to miss a pass may in the end lead to good playing. Collectively the acts of passing and receiving the ball have appropriate consequences, but the players do not respond in exactly the same way. This does not matter, however, as long as the action is effective enough and, of course, as long as the action is within the rules of the game. And this is where the analogy with football breaks down, for the rules of the football game are much more explicit and directive than the rules of the language loop and the conventions of general human communication. When it comes to the final result of the game, there is no question of a more-or-less win and therefore, when all is said and done, no way around passing a value judgement; however, as far as human communication in general is concerned, this is precisely the point: on the one hand there is never anything that can be characterized as *the* meaning, but on the other hand it is not the case that anything goes.

"What is crucial for reciprocality . . . is not the degree of *identity* of the participating elements, but the extent of their *congruence* or, it could be said, mutual 'fit'" (Smith, 1997, p. 67). Smith considers that pidgin languages provide an appropriate model, because in such languages verbal practices are stable enough to be effective in communication, while at the same time the meaning of certain terms cannot be explained with reference to one (original) version. In fact, the possibility of a mutual fit in social patterns arises precisely because interactions and communications have some stability over time. If only one version of meaning is experienced, it will be impossible to say whether this is a generally accepted meaning or not. It might be an aberration. With more meanings there are more possibilities, and because persons tend to respond broadly in more or less similar ways to a range of conditions, the different versions will overlap and be similar in some respects while not in others. Over time, with this kind of stability, patterns that are more or less similar and systematic emerge.

When Smith refers to the language loop, she is talking about how persons in communities, cultures, and social groups communicate, but family therapists also recognize the loop from their own communication with their clients. Good therapy is an ability to enter into a language loop with one's clients, and the question of how this can be done in family therapy has been written about in different ways. Minuchin wrote about joining (Minuchin & Fishman, 1981), Cecchin about neutrality (Cecchin, 1987), and the idea of "fit" has been central to the work of Maturana and Varela (1980) and their influence on family therapy thinking, and all these ideas owe a debt to Bateson's observation of information as "a difference which makes a difference" (Bateson, 1973, p. 457). This is the familiar problem of needing to do something different or unusual in the therapy-room, but at the same time what we choose to do should not be too different or too unusual, because this would lead to disintegration (Andersen, 1992). We aim to perturb, but not to disturb. The language loop—with the idea that patterns are always more-or-less patterns—encourages us to find confidence in this qualified uncertainty. It is a fact of all social and cultural life and of the human condition and is therefore a constructive starting-point for all communication. Most important of all, perhaps, the idea of the more-or-less pattern encourages us to ask questions when we thought we knew, and this is particularly important for cross-cultural work.

## *Non-rationality*

The third reason why a social system is different from a mechanical system relates to the way the system functions. If the thermostat does its job—that is, regulates the temperature and therefore functions in the way it was intended—we tend to think that this is good. With social and cultural systems, it is different. A social system can operate and different patterns be well coordinated without this telling us anything about the state of the persons who constitute it. They might be happy or unhappy. This we can only establish through a dialogue and interactions between them and us, and this happens over time. The mere functioning of a social system thus does not tell us anything about its value or about the nature of the premises on which the system is based. We might say that social systems are non-rational. That is to say, to talk about rationality or irrationality is simply besides the point (Shweder, 1984), because in social systems agents or persons participate in the more-or-less patterns that make up their social contexts, and it is this participation that gives them an understanding of themselves. It is not a question of whether the acts or communications of persons inside a system should make sense to those outside it, for persons—be they therapists or clients or anyone else—may be deluded, badly informed, confused, or negatively disposed (Taylor, 1985). It is this distinction that has been intensely debated in family therapy around the issues of violence, control, and power (Bateson, 1978; Berger, 1978; Dell, 1989; Goldner, Penn, Sheinberg, & Walker, 1990; Haley, 1976; Sluzki & Ranson, 1976). Haley, who can be said to have begun this debate with Bateson, vacillated between considering a quest for control (Haley, 1976) on the one hand, and benevolent concern (1980) on the other, as the motivation of individual persons for joining systems. But we can now see that the question of individual motivation is a much more complicated matter, which cannot be addressed by attributing universal validity to one or two premises that are in any case mainly derived from our own culturally constructed experiences. As the work of Fonagy et al. (1995) demonstrates and as we know as far as we ourselves are concerned: to start with, persons do not choose to participate in social and cultural systems. Persons are born or drawn into systems by the contexts and relationships around them, and on the occasions when there is a question of choice, the motivation for joining is always socially and culturally constructed and therefore more complex and more diverse than can be expressed by referring to a universal and generic human characteristic. It is by recognizing the interconnection between different parts or elements in systems and the motivation of individual persons as two separate issues that therapists can work with "both/and" (Goldner, 1992) and address violence and abuse in families safely.

## *Summary*

As a way of drawing together some of the ideas I have discussed, I shall summarize the argument so far. In this and the previous two chapters I have generally commented upon two ideas: "culture" and "system". I noted that there is a tendency for family therapists who consider themselves constructionist and/or narrative therapists to lose sight of the idea of "system". This is partly because of the association of systemic approaches with "objectivity" and "expertise", but also because of the contemporary emphasis on multiplicity and diversity. I have also argued that despite this not being clearly stated, cultural assumptions play a role in the therapist's use of techniques and her justification for these. I then described culture and its implication for social relationships by using Fonagy's revised model of attachment, and I suggested that because culture is a collection of interrelated patterns of meaning through time, culture is a kind of system. Culture is difficult to distinguish from social relations because it is only through relating to each other that persons share meaning. Finally, I have tried to clarify what kind of system we are talking about. This cultural and social system is a roughly defined collectivity of persons in which individual persons are connected to other persons through ongoing communication that implicates ideas about the way things should be done but is also sufficiently "more-or-less tuned" so that new ideas and new patterns can emerge over time. In this way, culture is a roughly defined collection of more-or-less patterns relating to the emotions, thoughts, behaviours, dreams, motivations, dispositions, orientations, and intentions of persons with no inherent objective apart from that which persons who participate in it might give it and which is presented to them as more or less the best way of doing things. I am not primarily talking about a complex academic paradigm, although culture and system are complex processes. Rather, I am suggesting that all persons operate with a view of themselves and others in more-or-less social patterns and, in this sense, with a rough and loosely defined idea of a system. In the face of the constructionist emphasis on heterogeneity and increased problematization, I have thus chosen to bring time, continuity, and pattern into focus because I think that this offers a possibility for the development of an ethically justifiable and cross-culturally sensitive therapeutic practice. In family therapy terms, I want to reintroduce process, but not without keeping a secure hold on content. This does not mean, therefore, that I think that family therapists should return to the days when the mechanical cybernetic system was the implicit model and the heterogeneity of social life was largely ignored. As everyone knows, this had oppressive and colonizing consequences. I think that great leaps forward have been made by emphasizing the social and cultural construction of knowledge, its local nature, and the right for it to be articulated and heard. However, there are dangers in this too, for if we abandon ideas of system, pattern, continuity, and process or if we leave these as implicit assumptions, unarticulated both to ourselves and others including our clients, then we are in danger of replacing (perhaps unknowingly) an abstract, explicit idea of "the system" with our own ideological and ethnocentric assumptions about the way things ought to be. This ethnocentricity will limit our ability to ask questions and could bring us back to a colonizing stance, even though this would be less obvious and less easy to identify. In the next chapter, I move towards a synthesis of the old and the new as a preparation for how these ideas may be applied in the practising of therapy.

CHAPTER FIVE

# Information and experience

I have pointed to two aspects of what therapists do in their work with clients. On the one hand, they interact, talk with, relate, co-construct, and generally try to connect; on the other, they use ideas, notions, models, and assumptions that derive from their own personal and professional backgrounds and contain material not wholly obtained during the encounter with a client. This knowledge and these experiences were acquired before—some during education and training, some derived from the early experiences of the therapist. Not all this knowledge is explicit. Some of it is implicit to such an extent that it seems to be "natural knowledge", or the only type of knowledge or experience about a certain event there could be. In this way, some of the knowledge may be barely accessible, although this of course depends on the therapist's training and her personal characteristics and ability to have insight about herself. Although these two modes always overlap and implicate each other, and it is only possible to make a distinction for the purposes of theory or analysis, we may consider them as moments (sometimes very short and fleeting) in which different types of understanding come into play. Walter Benjamin's distinction between information and experience cuts across these two modes of experience and is helpful.

Benjamin wrote about storytellers, and he recounts a story told by Herodotus about the Egyptian king Psammenitus (Benjamin, 1936). In this story, Psammenitus was captured by the Persian king Cambyses, who insisted on humiliating him to the utmost. He made Psammenitus stand by the roadside and watch as the Persian procession passed triumphantly. In it, Psammenitus saw his daughter being forced to walk as a lowly maid and his son prepared for execution. Although all the Egyptians wailed in distress at seeing this, Psammenitus stood unmoved, until the time when he noticed one of his servants, an old, impoverished man, walking along with the prisoners. Upon seeing this old man, Psammenitus broke down, beat his chest, and showed the signs of deepest mourning (Benjamin, 1936, p. 89). Having told this story, Benjamin goes on to point out that several different explanations of it are possible: one explanation, apparently offered by Montaigne, was that this king was already so full of grief that the smallest addition to this—that is, seeing the servant—caused his emotions to overflow. Other explanations offered by Benjamin are that "the king is not moved by the fate of those of royal blood because that is his own fate" or that "we are moved by much on the stage that does not move us in real life" (Benjamin, 1936, p. 90), or it could be that the king has had an especially meaningful relationship with this servant, and so on. It is, of course, this possibility of many meanings and explanations of which the narrative therapist makes much use, and a story can be told in many different contexts and at many different times while still keeping its power and strength (Dwivedi, 1997). A story communicates an experience, and whether one meaning or another is chosen will depend on the context and on who is listening. In a story, "The most extraordinary things, marvellous things, are related with the greatest accuracy, but the psychological connection of the events is not forced upon the reader" (Benjamin, 1936, p. 89).

The story, then, allows several different explanations, but it does not in itself offer one particular explanation. An explanation is what is placed on the story by the listener or even by the storyteller afterwards (Bruner, 1990). "It does not expend itself. It preserves and concentrates its strength and is capable of releasing it even after a long time " (Benjamin, 1936, p. 90). It is this quality of storytelling which lends itself to communication across different experiences, such as across different audiences, across cultures, and across clinical and non-clinical populations (Dwivedi & Gardner, 1997). But, for family therapists, therein also lies a danger, for the therapist and her clients must choose an explanation or perhaps a couple of explanations. The(se) explanation(s) opt(s) for one rather than another meaning, and this choice cannot exclusively be derived from the experience of listening to the story. It must also be derived from what has happened in each of their lives before. Thus Strathern (1999) quotes from a colleague anthropologist, James Wiener, who himself reported that when Naritjin, an Australian aboriginal artist, was asked to talk about the significance of a bark painting, he replied: "There are too many meanings. Later on, when you know more, you'll know which ones to choose and which ones to discard" (p. 46). This is where information comes in.

Family therapists are well acquainted with the idea of "information". Who has not heard of Bateson's definition (1973) of information as "a difference which makes a difference" or "news of a difference"? Trainees in family therapy continue to read Bateson's work. The enduring appeal of Bateson's ideas is pertinent to my argument, for Bateson has been described as a "maverick" (Ingold, 1986, p. 195) and as someone whose work is "typically unclassifiable" (Boon, 1999, p. 77); also, as I indicated earlier, Bateson was unique both in anthropology and in psychiatry because he wanted to bridge physical and social worlds (Harries-Jones, 1995). But this breadth of approach also holds its hazards, for such a connection is complex and complex ideas easily become reductivist in application. In view of the change from a mechanical to a social system in family therapy, should we not now also expect a reappraisal of "information" along the lines of the reappraisal of "power" which captivated family therapy some years back? (Berger, 1978; Dell, 1989; Krause, 1993; Sluzki & Ranson, 1976).

Bateson wrote several articles in which he discussed information, and those that have been on reading lists have tended to be those in which learning, communication, and logical types were discussed from a cybernetic perspective. With an emphasis on the system as a social system, we may approach these ideas from the point of view of art and the humanities. Art is, of course, directly relevant to culture, and Bateson also wrote about information from the point of view of art. I return now briefly to Benjamin and eventually back to Bateson in order to consider how to answer the question that was posed by Naritjin, the aboriginal artist: how do we choose one explanation or meaning rather than another? How are meanings discarded?

Benjamin agrees with Bateson: contrary to the story, which may be told again and again and still live on to captivate the listener, information does not "survive the moment in which it was new" (Benjamin, 1936, p. 89). This is because it "lays claims to prompt verifiability" and because we require it to "appear understandable in itself" (p. 88). Information does not allow suspense of understanding; it calls for an explanation and the choosing of a meaning. In short, it calls for an interpretation. Information pulls in knowledge that we already have and to which we can relate the news. In this way, information can never stand on its own, because the news of a difference must implicate the hidden, other part of the search: difference from what? Of course we may not be conscious of the "what", since this "what" may be derived from knowledge we have as a result of experiences of which we are not aware. Thus we never leave a difference simply as a difference, because the fact that we can identify it as a difference in the first place means that we must relate it to something else that we have, explicitly or implicitly, known about before. For human beings, no event can be outside meaning, just as we can never not communicate. But although we always communicate, we are not always successful in establishing the language loop.

Consider now how Bateson defines meaning; here, I quote from his essay on "Style, Grace and Information in Primitive Art":

> "Meaning" may be regarded as an approximate synonym of pattern, redundancy, information and "restraint" within a paradigm of the following sort: Any aggregate of events or objects (e.g., a sequence of phonemes, a painting, a frog, or a culture) shall be said to contain "redundancy" or "pattern" if the aggregate can be divided in any way by a "slash mark" such that an observer perceiving only what is on one side of the slash mark, can *guess*, with better than random success, what is

> on the other side of the slash mark. We may say that what is on one side of the slash contains *information* or has *meaning* about what is on the other side. [Bateson, 1973, pp. 103–104, emphasis in the original]

Here Bateson points to meaning as a systemic idea. Meaning is what has gone on before, because meaning depends on the capability of others to more-or-less anticipate what will be coming next. This is consistent with Smith's language loop discussed in chapter four, and it follows from this and from Fonagy et al.'s revised model of attachment outlined in chapter three that we use system to refer to "old" meanings. In this, more or less the same meanings have received more or less the same responses over time, so that they have become institutionalized. Think of "Christmas", for example. It is because there has been a pattern of meaning and action and because things and symbols have been imbued with these meanings that we more-or-less know and agree on what we are talking about. So, behind Christmas are social relations that over time have been manifest through persons acting and interacting in more or less the same ways. It has become a sort of routine. This is why I have defined "system" as persons connected to other persons and *connected to ideas about how things should be done*. And this last part of the sentence is important because we no longer think of a system as a collection of physical bodies. Rather, systems are collections of *persons* who are connected, and with them comes, willy-nilly, meaning—not added on like a belief system, but deeply implicated in conscious and unconscious thought and action.

So, from the point of view of the family therapist treating clients in therapy sessions, broadly speaking what comes after the slash mark is culture. Just as in his enquiry into art Bateson (1973, p. 105) placed his slash mark—"[characteristics of art object/characteristics of rest of culture]"—so the therapist may place "emotion", "husband", "bride", "dress", "child care", "respect", "nagging", and so forth on the right-hand side. In all cases, we are dealing with some kind of patterning, and the difficulty is to determine the nature of it. We know that it is not a reductionist one, because we know that whatever pattern we are talking about in social systems, it must be a more-or-less pattern, leaving room for individual variation that implicates culture without being determined by it. One challenge to the therapist, then, is how to acquire some kind of understanding of this patterning or, to put this in Bateson's terms, how to gain some understanding of the meaning of the (cultural) code rather than the meaning of the encoded message (Bateson, 1973, p. 103). This is difficult, and we all know that even Bateson himself sometimes had difficulties in keeping the distinction between the two levels in view.

I have suggested that here Benjamin's distinction between "information" and "experience" is helpful. This is because, as in Benjamin's story of Psammenitus, images, sentiments, experiences, and stories that emerge during therapeutic sessions offer the therapist the opportunity to gain some experience of the meaning of cultural codes. But she will also need to ask questions—or, rather, need to learn how to ask questions (Krause, 1998). The realm of experience in the therapy-room thus contains two opportunities for cross-cultural work. First, the possibility that the therapist may be able to join with the client, not by being the same as the client, but by connecting with some aspects of the client's experiences in the manner of Benjamin's story. This signals a common human predicament. Second, from this common ground arises the possibility that the therapist will be able to be curious about some of the less obvious aspects of the client's culturally constructed orientations. This in turn opens the possibility for obtaining new information that, when explained, may help open the way for new experiences and new ways of finding a common ground.

It is as well to remind ourselves that when we talk about more-or-less patterns, we must recognize that only some of the patterns, or only some aspects of the patterns, are conscious to the agents who are engaged in them. This is the case for our clients as well as for ourselves. No one can see the whole system or comprehend all the processes that affect her or him. This is not just because no one can see the whole picture, but also because persons are not aware of all that they do, nor do they know the meaning of all that they do. Whether this is a result of habit and routine sinking into deeper and deeper levels of the mind as Samuel Butler thought (referred to in Bateson, 1973, p. 108), or of processes of repression as Freud suggested, need not concern us here. What is important is to recognize that the processes of which persons are not aware are not only a result of something like "instinct" or "drive" or mammalian interaction, but also of culturally constituted patterns of interaction and meaning to which persons have been exposed from birth. Even before birth when the arrival of the infant is expected, others such as parents, carers, kinsmen and kinswomen, and so on behave, interact, and communicate with each other in culturally constituted ways that will affect the infant and each of those persons. Even when the infant is not expected, he is eventually born into a context in which infancy fills a particular social, cultural, and psychological space. Such unknown, unrealized, or unconscious experiences, regardless of their sources are referred to by Bourdieu (1990) as "doxic experiences", defined as

> the coincidence of the objective structures and the internalised structures which provides the illusion of immediate understanding, characteristic of the familiar universe, and which at the same time excludes from that experience any enquiry as to its own conditions of possibility. [p. 20]

These are experiences that a person takes for granted, because the conditions under which they are possible are not clear. Indeed, they cannot automatically be clear, because they are the background against which persons live their lives, interact with others, make decisions, and so forth. If they were always open for debate, action and decision-making would be difficult if not impossible. Thus, they mostly appear as "natural", even though they are socially and culturally constructed.

Bourdieu is a sociologist, an anthropologist, and a philosopher, and he is sceptical about the extent to which doxic experiences may be brought into the realm of consciousness (Jenkins, 1992). As therapists, we must see this differently. From our point of view, it is possible—indeed, it is part of our work—to facilitate making doxic experiences, or some of them, conscious, at least to the extent that these experiences can be reflected upon and, if need be, changed or understood in a new light. This is not a question of eliminating doxic experiences, for it is a fact of life that not all practice is consciously organized and that consciousness only holds a fraction of all mental processes (Bateson, 1973, p. 109). Rather, it is a matter of tracing those experiences and patterns, some of them doxic, that are implicated in the suffering and adversity experienced by the persons and the families we treat. In practical terms, this means that joining, understanding, and connecting are the first major therapeutic tasks in the treatment process and that in pursuing these the therapist is in charge of engaging clients around knowledge and experiences that they may not know that they have. How to do this respectfully and ethically (Raffin & Prata, 1998), particularly in cross-cultural work, is central to my concern, and I see a possibility for therapists to anchor their work in their own humanity and sociality in the manner suggested by Benjamin's "experience". This requires that therapists are alert to these aspects of themselves.

## *Guesswork and assumptions*

In view of our own partial knowledge of ourselves and the partial knowledge that our clients have about themselves, what of Bateson's guesswork in the passage quoted above? How can we, with more than random success, grasp the old meanings—that is to say, the patterns—from which the events or experiences that our clients bring derive meaning? And how can we do this when there are obvious cultural, linguistic, and social differences between us and our clients? To repeat, we cannot always ask our clients, because they may not necessarily know. Let me give an example.

It is by now well known that in different cultures persons may think about agency and personhood differently, and therefore, following Bateson, we may accept the following paradigm: [ideas about personhood and agency/characteristics of the rest of culture]. We need not here enter the debate of whether or not the difference between egocentric and sociocentric cultures (Shweder & Bourne, 1982) has been essentialized, although this is undoubtedly the case (Battaglia, 1995; Shweder, Much, Mahapatra, & Park, 1997). The question is how we can begin to ask families in therapy about these issues. We cannot ask, "what is your view of agency?" or "How do you see personhood in your culture?" If someone asked *us* this question, I doubt that many of us would be able to give a full answer. Of course, we could say something, but then I have phrased the question in terms with which most persons from

Europe or America will be able to connect. If translated into non-European languages, the question may simply not make sense and, even if it can be translated, it may be understood differently.

The question refers to material that in part in all cultures is doxic. In part, too, it therefore needs to be answered indirectly—that is to say, to access this material, different questions may have to be asked in order to enquire about issues that in some way are related to ideas about personhood and agency. This may vary in different cultures. Thus, in a seminal article the anthropologist Clifford Geertz (1973) wrote about this very topic in relation to Balinese culture. Geertz suggested that important cultural patterns must be understood contextually, and, to be able to describe the uniqueness of Balinese solutions to the problem of social as opposed to individual personhood, he needed to examine Balinese use of personal names, Balinese kinship terms, birth-order names, teknonyms (the practice of naming a person as a parent of a child—e.g. Father-of-Susan or Mother-of-Henry), titles, the Balinese calendar, and Balinese notions of time. Although a Balinese person would recognize the description of these topics, he or she would probably not be able to give the description of these patterns which Geertz provided. Of course, this description has a good deal of Geertz himself and his particular brand of anthropology in it too, but nevertheless the important point is that insiders rarely see the whole picture of their own existence and the social and cultural background to it, and the bits that are implicated in their own actions and agency may also be inaccessible to them. Now of course this did not mean that Geertz could not talk to Balinese persons. I do not know about Geertz's linguistic competence, but even if he spoke very little Balinese, he would still be able to communicate (through an interpreter if necessary) and interact with Balinese persons and in this way experience Balinese culture himself. This experience (whichever shape it took) was the first condition for the descriptions of Balinese personhood in his ethnography.

But most of us European and American family therapists do not think about personhood in this way—indeed, most of us probably have not thought about it at all. We might have subjected ourselves to various introspective processes, but that would have been a result of us taking for granted that personhood, agency, and consciousness is the way it is for us, naturally, for everybody. These are our doxic experiences, and we do not as a rule question the cultural and social conditions of their existence. Now if any of us were to live in Bali or somewhere else where we would get into close and prolonged contact with persons who act and think differently—and this is of course possible even within the United Kingdom—we would hopefully be open minded enough to eventually discover that the way we thought about ourselves is not the way everyone thinks. I say hopefully because this is by no means a foregone conclusion. As the murder of Stephen Lawrence and many other racist incidents show, it is possible to live side by side and be insensitive and murderously discriminatory about the way other people live, the way they look, and the way they think. I want to argue that the conditions for the making of ethical and respectful cross-cultural therapy do not come automatically and that it is not enough to point out differences. These conditions have to be consciously made and facilitated by the therapist. In this, the first step for the therapist is to identify her own assumptions and the areas in which her doxic experiences are implicated in mistaking for "natural" something that is, in fact, socially and culturally constructed. The therapist will therefore not be able to guess without first turning the questions onto herself—what are my own ideas of personhood, what do my own ideas about personhood say about my own culture, and, eventually which questions do I need to ask to find out how my clients see this?

## *Keeping "system" in mind*

There are, thus, things that the therapist can do and stances she can adopt that can help her join her clients to access the structures and conditions that are the background to their lives and their conscious and unconscious experiences. I discuss this further in relation to clinical material in the subsequent chapters. Here, I first want to take a step back and draw together what I have said so far with respect to the complaint made by the aboriginal artist regarding meanings and to what, following Bateson and Benjamin as well as others, I have called information and experience.

Experience is always embodied in the sense that experience implicates feelings, sensations, and imagery (Csordas, 1996). In this way, experiences with clients in therapeutic encounters are gifts to the therapist, but she can only use these fully after a certain amount of self-reflection. It is when patterns emerge in our experiences with our clients that we gain new information and knowledge. With this comes the ability to operate within Bateson's meaning paradigm and also, with time, the possibility of discarding meanings and choosing those that more or less fit. This is what family therapists call "joining" or "understanding" clients, and we can agree that as therapists we need to do this in relation to the client's (and not only our own) doxic experiences or background information. During this process, some experiences that were inaccessible to families and clients before come into view or fall into place among other patterns, and this may lead to changes, different views, different feelings, or different interactions. In this sense, "Truth *happens* to an idea. It *becomes* true, is *made* true by events" (William James, cited in Jackson, 1996, p. 4). This becoming or being made true occurs in family therapy in the same way as is reported to be the case for the people who consult diviners among the Bunyole in Eastern Uganda (Whyte, 1997); there, people suffering misfortune consult many diviners, each of whom may propose different causes and treatment, and in this way several possibilities for action are open. But once action is taken—and this, is, of course, inevitable if suffering is to be stopped or averted—some meanings are discarded while others are seen to more or less fit. When this happens, something new is learnt about the meaning and the patterning of events. But these additions are not discoveries of "objective truths out there", for they are made by us and our clients—that is to say, they emerge through processes of interaction and communication. Experience, then, is a condition for information and knowledge. It becomes information when we discard meanings, and when we knowingly or unknowingly choose in this way we also use some idea of "system" in the way I suggested in chapter two for Kogan and Gale's description of Michael White's consultation. That is to say, we carry with us some notion of the way our own social and cultural systems operate and the functions and interconnectedness of different relationships, and it is this notion that we bring into focus with our clients.

But it will not do, as I noted above, that the truth that is made or the patterns that emerge in our therapeutic sessions with families are merely those of the therapist. This would be abuse of power. The system that the therapist must keep in mind is that of the family or the client, and I suggested that the first step towards accessing this is to be aware of the socially and culturally constituted nature of one's own system and the patterns, traditions, moralities, routines, and expectations within it. I highlighted this because if therapists emphasize experience exclusively, there is a double danger. On the one hand, the general in the story or in the narrative may be mistaken for the specific. This may lead to stereotyping or to the use of category fallacies—that is to say, the asking of questions that are not valid for or have no meaning to those to whom the questions are addressed (Kleinman, 1987). On the other hand, the therapist's self-knowledge may remain unchallenged.

As therapists, we need information about ourselves and others and the skill to elicit it in both. I now want to suggest that the notion of "a system" I am advocating here is a tool to this end and also that this is indispensable in cross-cultural therapy. My "system" is a social system in which patterns rather than rules are the focus and where patterns are "more-or-less patterns" rather than rigid structures. The minimum requirements of such a system are that different parts are connected and that this interconnection is functional in terms of ideas about the way things should be done as well as open to be experienced by individual agents over time. One could say that my "system" amounts to a hypothesis about the necessary interconnectedness of persons in human systems, a hypothesis that is nothing more than a summary statement about what it is like to be human. It underlines the universality of kinship, attachment, agency, suffering, and the ongoing feedback and development in human verbal and non-verbal communication. But the hypothesis is not specific—it cannot be, for the patterns are more-or-less patterns and the functions in the system can take many forms. For example, kinship connections for any group of persons may be a result of shared genetic material, other bodily substances such as bone or blood, or traits or of the exchange of gifts. And such connections may be traced in a number of different ways: through both parents, through fathers, through mothers; or in one way for some purposes and in another for other purposes;

and so on. Or, as we have seen, the way that individuals see themselves as persons and the way that they consider their own abilities to act, change, and affect the contexts of their lives varies in different cultures. The hypothesis is thus a hypothesis that informs and contains, but it does not direct. It is (almost) wide open. Its main purpose is to remind the therapist of questions such as "How is this connected to that?" or "How does it work?"—not to dictate or manipulate. It is aimed at the meaning of the code, not at the meaning of the encoded message, although both levels are implicated in it.

Experience is one moment in the therapeutic encounter in which the narrative and the stories that clients bring touch the therapist. It is a connection between the bodies and between the persons in the therapy-room. If the therapist is facilitative, it is also a connection between persons as human beings. It requires skill in being open-minded and containing on the therapist's part to create this context. Information comes into play when the therapist tries to explain the experience, when she tries to understand. It is then that the therapist chooses one meaning and discards others on the basis of previous patterns. This requires skill in acknowledging that all human beings live in social systems of connectedness without surreptitiously and implicitly substituting one's own patterns of connections for those of the client's. The questions that the therapist asks will be different depending on whether the therapist, knowingly or unknowingly, uses her own experience of her own system as a reference point or whether she is able to critique this sufficiently to acknowledge "system" as a generic concept without making assumptions about the content or the meaning of the connections. The latter mode is more likely to encourage curiosity and open questioning (Cecchin, 1987; Selvini Palazzoli, Boscolo, Cecchin, & Prata, 1980), that is to say the asking of questions that generate more questions and therefore new experiences and more information.

The therapist thus ought to be irreverent (Cecchin, Lane, & Ray, 1992), but for irreverence as a therapeutic stance there is qualified support. This is because the therapist cannot be irreverent towards the system as a generic idea, for whichever way she looks at it, systems are the conditions for our existence, and the full extent of the way they work and the processes that affect our experiences will never be accessible, neither to clients nor to therapists. Cross-cultural therapeutic work—or, indeed, any therapeutic work—therefore also requires commitment, reassurance, and confidence, and to this extent the therapist always acts strategically (Dallos, 1997; Fruggeri, 2000; Mattingly, 1998). I return to this in the Appendix, in which I offer a strategy for cross-cultural work, but in the next three chapters I show how I use the ideas of "system", experience, and information in my own work with families and clients whose cultural backgrounds are different from my own.

*PART II*

# CROSS-CULTURAL CLINICAL WORK

CHAPTER SIX

# Connectedness and rationality

From the previous chapters it should be clear that a systemic view is not automatically culture-free. We have replaced our idea of a cybernetic (mechanical) system with a social system, and a social system cannot be perceived or examined outside the cultural themes and meanings that provide the reasons for persons in it to be engaged with each other. However, as I described in chapter four, it is a characteristic of a social system as a generalization that describing it does not implicate value judgements. The fact that persons are related does not tell us anything about whether these persons are happy or unhappy in their relationships. What can, then, be said to be a human condition or a human theme—and in this sense to be "culture-free"—is connectedness. In all social systems, persons are connected to each other and to general more-or-less patterns and ideas about how things should be done. And this also extends to things and artefacts that behind them have social relations. Social systems are therefore characterized by *relationality*, both in organization and in process. But connectedness cannot by itself explain information, because connectedness is a condition for culturally constructed processes of interaction and communication. The interaction and the communication cannot take place without relatedness or connectedness being there in the first place. There is a wide variety of ways in which persons can be connected to each other, just as there is a variety of ways in which certain tasks can be performed, but the variation is not infinite, because all the different solutions must meet the requirements of human conditions. Nevertheless, the existence of variety means that *relationality* must be distinguished from *rationality*.

Relationality, connectedness, and attachment are human predicaments. However, when it comes to a closer understanding of how these processes work, they cannot be considered as abstract, ahistorical, or acontextual aspects of humanness. This is because these terms refer to the processes described in Fonagy et al.'s revised attachment model and Smith's language loop (see chapter three), and they cannot take place outside historically, contextually, and culturally situated processes of interaction between persons. This is also the context in which these processes must be understood by the therapist. That is to say, these processes must be understood from the point of view of the descriptions that these interactions bear for the persons or agents involved in them. They must be understood from the client's point of view. We are not, therefore, talking about rationality in the sense of logical consistency (Taylor, 1985), because it can be difficult or even impossible to decide what is logical in cultural and philosophical traditions different from our own without at the same time taking the view that one tradition is superior to another. Here, I want to use a famous example to clarify this point.

A debate took place some years back in anthropology around the question of whether beliefs in witchcraft are rational. Evans-Pritchard, a well-known British anthropologist, described what seemed like a pretty illogical belief regarding Zande witches (Evans-Pritchard, 1937). The Azande are a Nilotic people, and during the early 1930s, when Evans-Pritchard lived with them, they held a belief that the powers of witchcraft can be inherited from a parent and that its presence can be proved by a post-mortem examination of the intestines. If at a post-mortem examination of a dead person's body a black substance was found in the small intestine, the person would be considered to have been a witch. This seems pretty straightforward. Yet the Azande did not perform post-mortems very often, and the question of whether someone was a witch or not was rarely settled, either in this way or at all. It was an issue that tended to be left open and ambiguous. Some commentators held that this showed that the Azande were irrational, because they did not follow their ideas through to the logical end in order to demonstrate something about the world and settle difficult matters once and for all (MacIntyre, 1970); however, others, including Evans-Pritchard himself, contended that this conclusion was invalid because it was based on the assumption that the Azande accept our Western rules of science. These do not apply, it was argued, because witchcraft is a mysterious and not a scientific phenomenon, and the two require quite different kinds of understanding. Even Western scientific explanations cannot explain all coincidences (Evans-Pritchard, 1937; Horton, 1970; Winch, 1970).

The Azande were doing what we and persons in all other societies do during the course of our lives: they were explaining the fact that misfortune, accident, and bad luck occur. We also suffer these things and we also try to explain them to ourselves and each other, so it is not difficult for us to understand the purpose that beliefs about witchcraft might have served for individual Zande men and women. This does not affect our view that we may not find explanations in terms of witchcraft satisfactory or rational. Our own explanations tend to take a different course, for in Western science there is little regard for what things mean to persons and more interest in the way things (generally) are; this requires a disengaged perspective, one that is more distant from the experiences of persons and the pragmatics of daily life (Taylor, 1985, p. 143). On this point, our notion of rationality differs from that of the Azande and is, some might want to argue, superior. Thus, when an epidemic of contagious pneumonia broke out in the villages in the area of Nepal in which I and my husband lived during my ethnographic fieldwork, we felt compelled to help obtain and administer penicillin. It would have been unethical and a betrayal of our friends to have declined to take such action. Local people also responded to this crisis by sacrificing goats and calling in spirit mediums with a reputation for healing, but I do not think that either I or my husband doubted which of the two was the more effective treatment, at least in the short term.

While the therapist may find herself in a similar position and call upon a detached notion of rationality based on modern scientific practice, either because a life may be in danger or because she is faced with a dangerous situation, this is also a point of view that may encourage the kind of collective failures referred to by Macpherson in his report on the Stephen Lawrence murder inquiry, because it does not particularly encourage the therapist to find out and understand the client's point of view. For most of the time, the understanding that the therapist seeks to achieve about her clients and her interactions with them therefore calls for a different stance. This is a stance that does not separate theory and involvement and is as curious about process and dialogue as about the end result. This may be found in the kind of understanding that Taylor (1985) has referred to as attunement, which he describes in the following way:

> We do not understand the order of things without understanding our place in it, because we are part of this order. And we cannot understand the order and our place in it without loving it, without seeing its goodness. ... Not being in attunement with it is sufficient condition of not understanding it. ... [p. 142]

Understanding as attunement is thus quite different from understanding as logical consistency. The former implies engagement, patterns that more or less fit, and attention to detail, whereas the latter implies disengagement, accurate rules, and attention to general principles. While the latter may be well suited to achieving understanding of physical nature, the former is probably a better way for achieving understanding of persons and their experiences of the cultural and social contexts and relationships in which they live. To understand how different beliefs and principles can be coherent, make sense, and provide good enough and acceptable explanations (i.e. be rational), the therapist must become attuned to the descriptions that her clients offer, even though she may not consider that these are logically consistent or rational. Attunement does not mean that the therapist must hold *her* views of her client, nor that she must hold no views or hold her own views lukewarmly. It means that the therapist practises tolerance—in the sense that she allows her clients to hold their views as passionately or as dispassionately as she might hold hers (Eagleton, 2000).

I want to illustrate, using a brief description of my therapy with a client, the difference between rationality/understanding as logical consistency and rationality/understanding as attunement. Alice, a young Nigerian woman of 18, had been in care since she was 6 years old, and she had been through many unsuccessful placements with foster carers and children's homes. All her placements had been with black carers or in homes with black staff, and in some of these she had felt blamed and emotionally abused. She was referred by her social worker, who was preparing Alice for leaving the care of her present foster-mother and beginning to live independently. At this point, Alice was becoming increasingly depressed, finding it difficult to go out, and generally losing her motivation for attending college and looking after herself. She was also becoming intensely preoccupied with what she called evil spirits, which she thought were inside her and which she believed her mother had sent to harm her.

Alice was the second eldest of three children and had one elder sister and a younger brother. Her mother, who was also Nigerian, had been diagnosed with a mental illness and had suffered from this illness for many years; her neglect and emotional abuse of her children had been the reason why they had all been placed in care. Alice's brother had been adopted, while Alice and her elder sister had been placed in different children's homes. At the time when Alice came for therapy, the three siblings had little contact with each other or with their mother. Their father, who was black British and whom Alice could remember, had died shortly after Alice had gone into care. Alice's elder sister had been diagnosed with the same mental illness that her mother was thought to suffer from. Alice was convinced that her mother was a witch, and this, together with her preoccupation with evil spirits and occasionally their voices and the presence of Alice's other symptoms, had almost convinced the referring agency and the concerned social worker that Alice was suffering from an inherited mental illness and that, if things became much worse, Alice would need to be admitted to an adult psychiatric unit. This was a well-meaning and concerned plan, but it was nevertheless an example of understanding as logical consistency, since in Western psychiatry beliefs in witchcraft and evil spirits are generally considered irrational.

When I saw Alice I was struck by how much sense her general outlook on life made against the background of her story. She remembered her mother as a "bad mother" who had not looked after her children in the past and who now also took no interest in them. Alice adopted a different name so as to try to protect herself from the evil spirits that her mother kept sending her way. Alice also gave the impression of being stuck and hopeless. She could not think about what needed to change or what she would want different, apart from being able to fight her mother's witchcraft more effectively. In our discussions about adolescent issues—clothes, boyfriends, girlfriends, going out, and so on—Alice emphasized the virtues of a balanced view and was not able to say much about what she herself wanted. She often said that "being unreasonable gets you nowhere" when I tried to find out about whether she was feeling angry or whether she wanted something different, such as a chance to go to college, or a chance to receive some more concentrated and sustained therapeutic help than I could offer her. Alice also asked me often if I believed in evil spirits and witchcraft.

It seemed to me that there was no discontinuity between the world that Alice described and a world in which witches and bad spirits abound. Against the background of her experience, she was being rational, although suffering and unhappy. I told her this, and witchcraft and how to combat it became the frame for our conversations. We talked about witches as grappling, selfish creatures, who take what they want, maybe to revenge wrong that has been done to them. We described them as thoroughly evil and unreasonable. We also talked about how witchcraft works in those societies in which it is generally accepted that witches exist. I did not mention the Azande to Alice, but certainly I had societies like the Azande or the Nupe of Northern Nigeria (Nadel, 1952) in mind. In such societies, the power of evil may be countered by antidotes, good spirits, or good people with special powers, so that things can be set right and life can go on. Of course, there are variations in different societies, but in general there is always the possibility of balancing evil with good, injustice with justice. Since Alice's own view was very much the opposite of the evil, inconsiderate, and selfish witch, underneath the layers of the evil spirits that she thought her mother had placed upon her she was a good spirit, and much of the therapy focused on how Alice could get in touch with and extend the work of this good spirit which was in herself. Alice liked this frame; she kept coming for quite a while and made some progress. She began to go out and attended the entire public inquiry into the murder of Stephen Lawrence; she also eventually agreed to a referral for more intensive therapy.

There were, of course, many issues that needed addressing for Alice, and in this my work with her was just the beginning. But Alice engaged, and I think she could do this because the themes that we made central in our meetings helped me attune to her suffering and helped Alice experience this attunement. Central among these themes were those of suffering and of parent–child or caring relationships (in Alice's case, these had all been broken). Both of these are pan-human themes or human conditions—that is to say, they signify what it is like to be human everywhere in all cultures and societies (Kirmayer, 1993; Kleinman & Kleinman, 1996). Because both Alice and I and everyone else have experienced these themes in some way, my participation in Alice's world could be conveyed through them. Furthermore, I could accept that although these conditions or themes are experienced by everyone, the content of that experience can be talked about, explained, and described in many different ways, and referring to witchcraft and evil spirits is only one way of addressing, processing, and explaining them. From this point of view, I could convey tolerance, even though I would not express or explain my own suffering in this way.

As the therapist, I chose a frame for the therapy. This frame was at the same time my hypothesis and the way I could keep "system" and connectedness in mind. It contained my assumption regarding the necessary characteristics of the social systems in which Alice and I both existed, namely that children need positive experiences of the relationships they have with those who take care of them and, if these experiences are negative, there is likely to be suffering. This assumption was a general one, and I also made it explicit with such statements as "You have had a hard time" or "Life has not been fair to you", although I did not elaborate. This hypothesis suggested something about human beings in general and helped me show Alice that I wanted to understand. It is similar to what Minuchin (1999) has recently referred to as a universal truth (p. 10), and tolerance and attunement as a philosophical outlook are, I think, also implicated in his notion of "joining" (Minuchin & Fishman, 1981), just as they must be in ethnography, which as a research method aims to understand cultures and societies from the point of view of those who live in them (Krause, 1998). In this sense, joining or attuning is not a stance but an ethical position, and it implies joining with the meaning of the client's descriptions as this appears to him or her as much as joining with the client as a person. Indeed, the two cannot be considered to be separate. In order to become attuned with Alice's experiences, I needed to address the issue of witchcraft and evil spirits, not as a way of tricking her into a dialogue with me, but as a genuine and valid—some would say rational—response to suffering. Alice and I entered the language loop because we were talking about more-or-less the same issues in a way that could more-or-less be understood by both of us.

Yet the concern of Minuchin's critics are legitimate, because it was crucial that one description was not considered more true than another (Anderson, 1999) and that my hypothesis about human conditions did not become a gloss on Alice's particular situation (Combs & Freedman, 1998). My hypothesis had to leave open how different details of Alice's life were connected to other details and what sense she made of these. These details could only be settled by asking Alice questions, talking to her, and being with her during the therapy. My hypothesis provided a frame for my exploration of the detailed content and processes that, as a therapist, I needed to begin to understand if Alice was to gain anything from our meetings. It did not seek to substitute something universal for something particular. With this idea of system, then, I declared a point of view. This point of view was a view about human beings in general, informed by what I know about different cultures and societies, both my own and those of others. It was a view of the issues or conditions that people in all societies and cultures must address, face, and in a collective sense survive. These include suffering (from death, sickness, accident, or misfortune), connectedness (kinship or other social connections), physical growth, life-cycle issues, personal transformations, agency and embodiment (the experience of oneself as embodied), and of course the reflexive processes in the language loop, which in themselves are conditions for social existence, because no human being can exist by him/herself. To refer to these human conditions is not to evoke a thoughtless universalism. Rather, it is to challenge the therapist to go beyond her own culturally constructed ideas and inclinations in order to join her clients in a foothold from where particulars can be explored. It is a strategy or a tool that aims to help therapist and client access and eventually choose some meanings while discarding others. It is also an ethical position because it aims to avoid that the philosophical stance of *not knowing* (Anderson, 1997; Anderson & Goolishian, 1988, 1990) or "the view from nowhere" (Nagel, 1986) is inevitably countered by *a view from us alone* (Eagleton, 2000). It is thus not a question of the contextual constraints of the therapy giving the therapist freedom (Minuchin & Fishman, 1981, quoted again in Minuchin, 1999, p. 11). It is, rather, that the freedom of the client *depends on* the therapist acknowledging, first, that systems cannot be without meaning and, second, that meanings are more-or-less patterns and always carry ambiguity or polysemy. In cross-cultural work, but in intra-cultural work too, it therefore falls to the therapist to approach meaning in as disciplined and ethical manner as is possible, and this discipline starts with the therapist examining the extent to which her own views and meanings are socially and culturally constructed. This is closely implicated in how the therapist tunes in to her client's point of view. Nothing is culture free, but we can attempt to go beyond our own cultural constructions by being consistent and clear in our questioning of them. In summary, then, in my work with Alice this process took the following course.

I began, as I always do, with the assumption that the social system around Alice, which she had experienced, had influenced her view and feelings about relationships and the world. I do not remember sharing this general view with Alice, but, as I describe in the next chapter, I often do share thoughts of this kind with families. My experience during my conversations with Alice pointed me towards explanations of misfortune and suffering as one of Alice's preoccupations. I did not follow the view of my own cultural tradition that this is irrational, even though this was not to say that I did not think that Alice was suffering upset or something else that by some might be glossed as "mental illness". Instead, I assumed a relatedness between the meaning of Alice's experiences and the meaning of what she was telling me. This informed my questions to her—"How does it work with the evil spirits?", "When do they come?", "How do you know that they are there?", "What would your mother's mother or your aunt advise you to do?", "How can you fight evil?", "Can someone give you an antidote?"—and my connecting with her experience—"You have had a hard time", "Some good spirits must have protected you from becoming completely destroyed", "Despite your experiences you are on the side of 'good'." These conversations generated information about how Alice might be able to fight the evil spirits, and this is similar to White's idea (1989) and practice of externalizing. It is important, however, that this process was not just considered as one person's challenge to a Western cultural view, that I did not simply consider Alice as an agent free to choose and to combat the dominant Western philosophical view that places personal characteristics inside rather than between persons. It was necessary that it took place using the rationale of the system and the world view which Alice herself was putting forward. In this view, both good and evil spirits were externalized. Externalizing as a technique must be culturally isomorphic, and it just so happens that most cultural traditions do not share our professional theories and Euro-American egocentric views on this matter.

Now there might be this objection: as someone whose first training was in social anthropology, I am familiar with many different cultural traditions regarding the explanations of misfortune, suffering, and illness and, of course, just as is the case for anyone else, my previous training informs the assumptions I make and my practice. However, I also think that family therapists can learn to be alerted to issues of this kind. So, for those who have not thought much about the difficult problems regarding rationality and who have never heard of the Azande, I suggest that you stop at the point when you think that without further questions you can explain what is going on. In my work with Alice, this point was when Alice first spoke about evil spirits and witchcraft to me, and I had to wonder what these ideas might explain to her.

CHAPTER SEVEN

# Choosing meaning: 1

Witchcraft and evil spirits may seem exotic to us, but in a sense because of this fascination these issues should cause few problems in therapy. If the therapist is able to start from the idea of the non-rational and from the assumption that all kinds of ideas have a function to those who hold them, then further exploration will be possible. With Alice, I followed a line of what can be called ethnographic questions in order to understand how her system—which included not only disrupted care relationships but also good and evil spirits—worked. It may be harder to do this when the line of enquiry concerns ordinary and less obviously different ideas from those we ourselves may hold.

In this chapter, I pursue the notion of asking ethnographic questions. I refer to them as ethnographic because these questions are very similar to those I might ask as an ethnographer in order to acquire an understanding of a particular local and cultural world and the way this forms a background to the lives of the people in it (Krause, 1998). My questions here concern matters (such as mourning and relationships) that are perhaps more familiar to Western family therapists. I have chosen material from the beginning of a course of therapy (a third session) because this is typically when the therapist begins to comprehend what it is she must aim to understand in order to help facilitate a change. My emphasis is on how meanings emerge and are chosen, and again the "system" that I keep in mind to start with is a notion of general human conditions. During the therapy, this is slowly replaced by a comprehension of the system of social relationships and meanings that form the background to the lives of the members in one particular family.

Anna, who was 14 years old, was referred with her father's ex-wife. She had been truanting from school and was also difficult to manage at home. Anna is Brazilian, and she had come to live with her father's ex-wife Isabella, in London, with her younger sister, Maria, who was 13 years old, after their father was killed in a car crash and their mother had died of cancer. This was two years before the referral. Isabella had two children from her marriage to Anna's and Maria's father: a son, Pedro, and a daughter, Cecilia. Cecilia, who had married and herself had a child, also helped her mother look after her half-sisters. Pedro was 25 years old and still lived with his mother; he was also the legal guardian of his half-sisters. Isabella was very worried about Anna, her education, and the fact that she was withdrawn and did not seem to enjoy life very much. She was not so worried about Maria.

It was clear what Isabella wanted from the referral: help for Anna, so that Anna could get on with her life and her education. It was also clear that the two girls had endured a terrible tragedy, and it was possible that the way Anna was feeling was connected to these events. Anna and Isabella came on their own to the first session, and Anna had tears in her eyes when I asked questions in order to understand what had happened. But her life in school was also at risk. I therefore spent most of the first session addressing the school issue; in the second session, I addressed the school issue again, this time with Maria present. During this session we referred to, but did not spend much time on, the death of the parents. The extracts below are from the third session, and Isabella, Anna, Maria, and myself are present. We have just talked about how things are in school, and Anna has told me that she has taken more responsibility and Maria and Isabella have both helped her in ways that we had discussed in the previous session:

*Britt Krause*: I wanted to talk about something else. You know that Isabella is often saying here about the responsibility and how she feels responsible for you and she feels that she has a lot on her plate and sometimes when she shouts it is because she has your best interests at heart. And . . . I was wondering because you two have . . . you two have an unusual background, don't you? Not everyone has lost their parents the way you have. Not everyone has had to come to a different country to live . . . with new people, in new circumstances. . . . So how do you . . . how does it work? Do you call Isabella "mummy"?. . . . What do you call her?

*Anna*: We call her Auntie.

*BK*: Who decided that you would call her Auntie?

*Maria*: In fact in Brazil . . . she is my dad's ex-wife and we used to call her Auntie, so like it is the same thing.

*BK*: Right . . . right.

*Isabella*: Because in Brazil everybody calls everybody Auntie and Uncle.

*Maria*: If there is a bus driver . . . we call him uncle (*laughs*).

*Isabella*: It is a like, anybody who are found in the street we call him "Uncle" and "Auntie". I only saw them twice when they were little. Once when I went to Brazil and their father he said: my wife would like to meet you is that possible? Yes . . . come . . . So I came and met his wife. We meet and I meet the girls . . . I never saw them . . . I saw them only twice. When my son went there and he ask me if he can come with them. I was frightened . . . like them . . .

*BK*: You were frightened . . . ?

*Isabella*: Yeah, I think they did not know me, I did not know them. So you see . . . I was . . . I think everything went fine.

Here I introduced something I wanted to find out more about, something that I thought would be relevant and which I thought they could think about with a general statement, a hypothesis, an assumption about a system. This was the following: Anna's and

Maria's family circumstances are very unusual; most young people live with someone who is in a relationship of a mother or a father to them, but in this area of their lives they have had a loss and a change; I want to find out about their relationship to Isabella. This is the system I had in mind, but I did not know how this worked for them, and this is why I asked: how does it work? This is an ethnographic question, but it is not completely open. It would have been too difficult if I had asked: "What is your relationship to Isabella?" I do not think that I myself could answer such a general question in a meaningful way. So I asked about whether the girls call Isabella "mummy", and this was followed by another question, one could say a subquestion: who decided? I found out that Isabella is "Auntie", but also that this is a general term of address in Brazil. This is news (information) to me because although both in Denmark and England "aunt" and "uncle" may be inclusive kinship terms of address, Danes do not use this term so inclusively. Of course, I did not know how to use this bit of information. The session continues:

*BK*: But I wanted to talk about it because you know . . . it is always a little bit different, I think, or maybe it is different in Brazil, I don't know, but you know when you are not looked after by your natural parents and you are being looked after by someone else who is connected but not quite your natural parents, then sometimes there is this issues about . . . how about responsibility. You know Isabella has taken responsibility. She is saying I am responsible. . . . But how does it work for you, because you know that Isabella is not your . . . your natural mum.

*Maria*: Hmm . . .

*BK*: How does it work?

*Maria*: I think . . . like . . . after a time . . . because it is two years now . . . so the situation now . . . you kind of get used to it. So she looks after us as if she was our mum . . . so like . . . it will never change, our mum was our mum . . . we still remember our mum . . . and . . . things can't change. But those people they have babies and they have their own mums and they have a step-parent or something like that, I think it is the same thing, they treat them like their mum, but they know that they are actually not their mum. So I treat her like she was my mum, even though she is not my mum.

*BK*: What do you think, Anna?

*Anna*: Yeah, the same. . . . I consider her my mum . . . yeah the same.

*BK*: Hmm. . . . So what happens to the idea of your . . . real . . . mum?

*Anna*: Yeah . . .?

*BK*: Does it come up?

*Anna*: (*reluctantly*) No . . .

*Isabella*: (*tuts loudly*) . . .

*BK*: Do you think of her?

*Anna*: I used to.

*BK*: You used to. . . . When did you used to think of her?

*Anna*: Oh, . . . a year ago . . .

*BK*: What time . . . in the night? . . . in the daytime?

*Anna*: All the time . . . like during the day . . . and the night and things . . .

*BK*: You used to think of her all the time?

*Anna*: Yeah.

*BK*: What did you used to think when you thought of her?

*Anna*: Hmm. . . . When she was dying . . . yeah that is the only picture I can get . . . yeah.

*BK*: In your mind . . . so it is a sad picture?

*Anna*: Yeah . . .

*BK*: How did it stop. . . . How did it stop that she was in your mind so much?

*Anna*: Well, I don't know, how it was . . . I just started enjoying more by myself. . . . I started like listen to what people said to me . . . and you know . . . trying to cooperate as well . . . if like around my house and so on . . .

*BK*: Aha. . . . (*to Isabella*) Did you notice that change from when Anna stopped thinking so much about her mum?

*Isabella*: Yeah. . . . I think she tried . . . she tried to be something else . . . somebody else. . . . Anna, you try to forget, but you never forget. I lost my mum 51 years ago . . . she died on 22 February in 1949. I still remember the day she died . . .

*BK*: You too were a child?

*Isabella*: I was four years old so I still remember the day she was in the coffin to go to the cemetery, you know. That picture is here in my mind . . . so don't try to put her aside, Anna. You must remember, she is your mum, you understand. And don't remember only the bad things, remember the good things, the times she was there for you when you went to school, when you come home she give you food, she give you a kiss, something like that. I don't remember much because I was only four years old. So the only thing I remember . . . once someone tried to hit me, I don't know . . . I ran and I hold her legs, you know, like a child do, something like that . . . and I remember when she died, my brother was born and she died eight days after that . . . so . . . the only thing I remember. . . . Don't forget your mum, it is your mum . . .

*Anna*: Yeah . . .

*Isabella*: Don't put her aside. . . .

*BK*: Are there some things you can remember from before she was ill?

*Anna*: (*in a low voice*) Yes . . .

*BK*: What can you remember?

*Anna*: After school when I used to come home . . . and . . . (*pause*) that is all . . .

*BK*: Hmm . . .

*Isabella*: I think it is hard for them, because she was ill for two years. . . . No?

*Anna and Maria*: Yes . . .

*Isabella*: She was very ill and they did not even find out that she was with cancer till she was almost dying, so I think it was hard for them . . .

*Maria*: The doctor did not tell her that she had cancer as well . . .

*Isabella*: So she was always ill . . . you know . . . so . . . you know.

*BK*: What about you Maria? Do you have . . . do you remember her?

*Maria*: Yeah, I do.

*BK*: What do you remember?

*Maria*: Like I used to go on Mondays when I got home from school . . . and . . .

*Anna*: (*laughing a little*) Yeah . . .

*Maria*: And like we were watching soaps on the TV, and on Sundays, we did not do anything, we just stayed and watched TV and like that . . .

Again I proposed a general predicament—that is, not being looked after by one's biological parents—and then I asked how this works for Anna and Maria. But this time I was highlighting a different aspect of relationships between children and mothers, namely taking responsibility and accepting authority. This was a deliberate choice on my part. Instead of following Isabella's statement by asking about how she coped, I left this for later. I had not yet finished finding out about the way Anna and Maria see the relationship between children and mothers, or persons who care for them as mothers. This is, of course, connected with the way they see their relationship to Isabella and to their dead mother—that is to say, they only know about the general through their own particular experience. I was not repeating myself when I asked again: "How does it work?" Nor was I insisting that we talk about this in my way. I was opening up these issues for an exploration from a different point of view, because these issues have many aspects and can be seen from many different angles. I was being curious about the ideas of giving and receiving mothering and care which the persons in this family have, because if I were going to become attuned to Anna, Maria, and Isabella I had to understand their involvement with each other as comprehensively as possible.

This strategy of exploring something from different points of view is an ethnographic strategy that Geertz, somewhat paraphrasing Gilbert Ryle, referred to as "thick description" (Geertz, 1973). Thick description means the description of how a theme or issue may be implicated in different experiential contexts. It is important to notice that the meaning given to this idea both by Geertz and by Ryle is different (almost the opposite) from the meaning that seems to be attributed to it by some well-known family therapists (Minuchin, 1998; White, 1997). Geertz's emphasis, and the one I want to highlight here, is on how cultural themes (these are like Bateson's patterns) may be articulated in different contexts by individual persons and how through each articulation meaning is added to this theme. It is how you can see the same theme or same idea (complex of ideas) from different points of view. Thick description emphasizes continuity. It is thus not simply the adding of different versions of stories, or different persons' versions of the same story, on top of each other the way one might add one layer after the other to make a cake and the way Minuchin (1998, p. 402) describes White's use of this idea. The difference is crucial. While White may be concerned with deconstruction and complexity (White, 2000), Geertz and Ryle were also concerned with constraint on diversity and, most importantly for my purposes here, with continuity, since thick description requires that one keeps the theme or the idea in mind. And, of course, "thick description" for Geertz and Ryle is a theoretical tool or a construct, not something that can be described as actually existing on the ground. It is something that the therapist or the ethnographer constructs, not what clients or informants do or even necessarily experience. I suspect that Minuchin, too, would find this original notion of "thick description" useful.

My main question about how not being cared for by a "natural" mum works was followed by a number of subquestions that are responses to the responses of Anna, Maria, and Isabella to my original question. These questions tracked what their mother means to the girls now, two years after her death and when they are with a different "mother". "What do you think?" "Does it come up?" "Do you think of her?" "What time?" "What did you used to think when you thought of her?" "How did it stop?" During this sequence, Anna and I were in the language loop since we were talking and experiencing more or less the same things (remember, the language loop is not only about language). This is perhaps similar to what DiNicola has called spiralling (DiNicola, 1997, p. 40), except that I consider that my keeping the idea of system in mind and the general theme of mother/children alive allowed Anna, Maria, and Isabella to lead me towards the particulars of their situation. I was not simply being led by them, because this would have been too difficult for them and it would also not have helped them to begin to think about these issues in what might be a new way. Their particular answers were explicit responses to my general statements, but I was consciously trying not to let these statements reflect only my own points of view; rather, I was trying to express and think about them so that they articulated general human conditions and the systemic aspects of the lives of all human beings.

Two bits of information or two patterns emerged from this sequence, not just to me but also to Anna, Maria, and Isabella. First, Anna's preoccupation with the sad memory of her dying mother and her reaction to this. Hearing Anna talk about this made Isabella tut loudly. Second, the similarity between Anna and Maria on the one hand and Isabella on the other: all three had lost their mothers when they were children. This opened up the possibility for Isabella to reaffirm Anna's and Maria's special relationship to their biological mother. "Don't forget your mother," Isabella says. Why do I consider these two sequences significant? In part this is because of Isabella's expressive use of language when she tutted. Isabella's tut was an example of how a "meaningless" sound can be very meaningful. Her utterance did not refer to an external aspect of reality, it was not referential; rather, it was a reaction to what Anna had said, and it drew our attention to Isabella (Briggs, 1996). It is an example of what Bateson called metacommunication (Bateson, 1973). It was a moment of insight, a moment in which Isabella knew what Anna felt and said and in which she tried to shape its discursive effects. It was a moment in which Isabella confirmed her participation. Although I noticed the tut and although "tutting" is familiar to me, I could not be sure what it meant. This was only clarified later when Isabella talked about her own experiences of losing *her* mother. These sequences provided information because they explained something about the situation and the relationships between Isabella, Anna, and Maria. They helped me towards choosing some meanings and discarding others. They also helped to raise new questions.

*BK*: Hmm. . . . What . . . do you think she [your mother] would think if she could see you now?

*Maria*: I think that she would be happy and sad at the same time.

*Anna*: I think she would be disappointed with me . . .

*BK*: Disappointed?

*Isabella*: (*exclaims*) Why? Anna?

*Anna*: I don't know . . .

*Maria*: If you think she would be disappointed why don't you try to do your best? Try to get better . . . then like if some day . . . like you could see her she would not be disappointed in you because you have tried to do your best, but . . .

*Anna*: Yeah, but I do . . .

*Maria*: (*interrupting Anna*) Why don't you try . . .

*BK*: Why do you think she would be disappointed . . .

*Anna*: I don't know, it seems like I always do something wrong . . .

*BK*: Does it?

*Anna*: Hmm. . . . Yeah. . . . I think so.

*Maria*: Yeah, but why don't you try to do it better? If you know you are doing something wrong, don't do it . . .

*BK*: Do you think you are doing something wrong? You said it seems . . . is that what you think? That you have done something wrong?

*Anna*: Yeah . . .

*Isabella*: I think she has the complex that she is bad, she is a bad girl. But she is not. . . . I do not know what is wrong with Anna.

*BK*: But you know you have just come today and told me that you have done something good, haven't you?

*Anna*: (*with a more definite voice*) Yeah, yeah . . .

*BK*: Do you think bad about that too?

*Anna*: (*in a lower voice*) No . . . no . . . that is good . . .

*BK*: That is good. . . . So if you mother heard that . . . what do you think she would say?

*Anna*: Yeah, she would probably be happy for me for doing the right things, you know. . . .

*BK*: What would she advise you to do, do you think? If you said to her "you are going to be disappointed in me because I am not doing things well", what would she advise you to do, do you think?

*Anna*: I don't know, I think she would try to say, you know, "now try to help yourself out", like . . . of course . . . like help myself, but help other people as well, like to cooperate with them . . . like, not just them trying to cooperate with me even though I do not need them to cooperate with me . . . yeah I think that would be it . . .

*BK*: Hmm. . . . Was she a religious person, your mum?

*Anna*: Yeah, yeah . . .

*BK*: She was?

*Anna*: Yeah . . .

*BK*: Did you used to go to church?

*Anna*: Yeah. . . . I did not go that much . . . I did not like church that much, but she used to go every Sunday .

*BK*: Right . . . right . . . so about school what might she say?

*Anna*: Hmm . . . about school? I don't know . . . I don't know . . .

*BK*: You don't know what she would say?

*Anna*: No, I don't know . . .

*BK*: Hmm. . . . So . . . (*to Maria*) . . . what do you think she would say?

*Maria*: About?

*BK*: About this situation, about this . . . what do you think she would say about you two?

*Maria*: About my sister she would be a bit disappointed, she would want my sister to get a bit better, because she does not try, you know . . . and about me, I think she would try . . . like make me, like more secure by myself, because I feel like weird by myself, you know, like I am scared of losing everything. I am always afraid of losing stuff.

*BK*: Hmm. . . .

*Maria*: So I think she would say, like you do not need to be afraid of losing this and that, because you are not . . . but I keep thinking "oh, I will probably lose this and then I will lose that" . . .

*BK*: You mean things?

*Anna*: Yeah, that is why she gets stressed out . . .

*Isabella*: Boyfriend, eh, Maria?

*Maria*: Yeah, that is one of the things as well . . .

My question shifted to another aspect of the relationship between Anna and Maria and their mother when I asked, "What do you think [your mother] would think if she could see you now?" This was followed by more subquestions: "If your mother heard you had done something good what do you think she would say?" "Was she a religious person?" "What do you think she would say?" This sequence repeated the pattern of the previous sequence. Anna's answer was further information, not just to me but also to Isabella and Maria as well. Both used expressive language, Isabella by exclaiming "Why?" and Maria by interrupting Anna. This time, Maria was also asked, and her response gave new information about how she had reacted to her mother's death and what she felt is wrong now. A bit later, this allowed us to talk about Anna and Maria as different and to consider that they both, not just Anna, had some problems. Isabella also talked about Maria as being "just like her father". I picked this up in another sequence in which I stuck to my aim of generating a "thick description" of Anna's, Maria's, and Isabella's ideas, attitudes, and thoughts about the girls' biological mother and the relationship of mothering.

*BK*: Can I just ask you what do you think that . . . your mother would say about the way that . . . because it is interesting isn't it, you know, that in some ways Isabella is right that, you know, that we do take characteristics from our parents, you know, I mean like . . . do you look like your mum? Who looks like your mum?

*Maria*: I do . . . a bit . . . like my mum and a bit like my dad . . .

*Anna*: No . . .

*Maria*: . . . and she is a bit like my mum . . . and a bit like my dad . . .

*BK*: Which bit of Anna is like your dad and which bit is like your mum?

*Maria*: Like my dad? . . . The eyes . . . like my dad . . . like the shape, . . . hmm . . . the nose is a bit like my dad and my mum. It is mixed because my mum had a nose like that here (*points to her nose*) and my dad had a nose . . .

*Isabella*: No, you are . . .

*Anna*: No . . .

*Isabella*: You are your father, she is neither mother nor father . . . she is not . . . she is a . . . you are like your father more . . .

*Anna*: No, I did not think that I look like that . . .

*Isabella*: No, I knew him when he was six, seven years old, so I grew up with your father you understand? . . . so . . . just the colour of the eyes is different . . .

*Maria*: Yeah?

*BK*: (*pointing to Anna*) Which bit has she got from her mum?

*Isabella*: The colour of the hair . . . and the eyes, but it is not. . . . Anna is Anna.

*Anna*: (*laughs*) . . . Yeah . . . (*laughs*)

Isabella introduced the idea of resemblance between parents and children. This is, of course, central to the theme we are exploring. I therefore follow her lead:

*BK*: But anyway you know we still get something physical from our parents, we do not know what and it is a mixture . . . and then there is this thing that you know, Isabella is here looking after you as your Auntie, as your new mother.

*Anna*: Yeah. . . .

*Maria*: Yeah. . . .

*BK*: And she has also done that for other people, because I remember last week you told me. . . . So what do you think your mother would say that you should take from Isabella, because Isabella . . .

*Maria*: I think it is her courage . . .

*Anna*: Everything she says . . .

. . . . . .

*BK*: (*to Isabella*) Do you think that they should take everything. . . . I mean I am not saying that they should not follow your rules, but you know . . . as a mother, which is also what you are to them, as a mother . . . you know . . . there are some things which you want your children to hang on to that you give and there are some things that you are not very proud of yourself that you have . . . you know everyone has bad and good things about them. What things? . . . I mean do you think that they should just copy you?

*Isabella*: No . . . no . . . I don't.

*BK*: They should not . . . ? (*turning to Maria and Anna*) So what do you think it would be important to keep?

*Maria*: Her courage . . .

*BK*: Isabella's courage? . . . What do you think Anna?

*Anna*: Hmm . . . yeah, her courage . . . her strength. . . . hmm . . .

*Maria*: Her guts . . . as well.

*Anna*: Yeah, yeah . . .

*BK*: Her guts . . . what do you mean by this?

*Maria*: Like she has . . . someone asks her to do something and it is quite dangerous she has the guts to go and do it.

*Anna*: Like it was not, like I bet it was not easy, like, to take care of two persons the daughters of her husband from another woman . . .

*BK*: Yes . . .

*Maria*: So she had the guts to come and take care of us. She did not feel scared or jealous or afraid . . .

*BK*: How do you think she did manage that, because I agree, you know when you first came here, I thought well here, you know there are so many people who marry and marriages break up and they marry again and they are jealous and they cannot get on . . . and here is Isabella not only getting on but actually agreeing to have you. How do you think she did it?

*Maria*: I do not know . . .

*BK*: (*to Isabella*) How did you do it?

*Isabella*: Well, I think nothing to do with anything. . . . I was so . . . my heart was crying for them. Not something which happens everyday you know. . . . I don't know . . . see . . . I love them . . . it is like they are mine. . . . I think I have to have more children . . . I have only two, I did not want any more children . . . so I think these two they were supposed to be mine . . . because everything happened like it was planned . . . God placed them . . . you understand. . . . I wanted to buy a flat, a house a long time ago and suddenly everything was possible. I bought a flat, I just moved in and their father die, my daughter has a baby the same day my ex-husband die and then my son went to Brazil and came with them. I think everything was planned, you see, I am a very religious person. . . . I don't go to church very much in the past, but I believe in God, you know . . . so . . . I don't know . . . I don't know how to explain. I know sometimes it is hard for me because I just bought a flat so it was time for me to rest and not work so hard for all my life I have worked very hard and now I have two more . . . more girls to feed . . . so . . . I am happy, you see . . . I feel comfortable with me. So if I said "no" that time when my son asked me, my conscience . . .

In these last extracts my questions were directed at Anna, Maria, and Isabella reflecting on and understanding their own system—that is to say, the connections between them and the meaning of these connections. I kept this system in mind, but I cannot say that I fully understood it. I cannot close the matter down. I have, of course, chosen some meanings and I think that I understand something, but there will always be more meanings and new meanings. This sequence began with the idea of physical resemblance between parents and children and moved to the idea that if persons care for each other and are connected by social connections and love, these connections mean that they will influence each other, be tied together, and build up some kind of resemblance. I had in mind that kinship connections need not be considered to be based on biological connections (Krause, 1998; Strathern, 1999). Hence my question, "What do you think you should take from Isabella?" But this question took us first to Isabella's motivations, intentions, and generosity, and the meaning of what Isabella said is an important basis for building these connections.

*BK*: So what do you think your mother . . . I mean if your mother could see, you can imagine that there would be some part of her that would be very sad, because she should be in Isabella's shoes . . .

*Maria*: Hmm . . . hmm . . .

*BK*: And she is not, she is not here, but what do you think that she might say to you that you should take from Isabella? . . .

*Anna*: I don't know . . . I don't know.

*BK*: You said her courage or Maria said her courage . . . but would your mother have said that?

*Anna*: Yeah . . .

*BK*: She would? . . .

*Anna*: Yeah . . .

*Maria*: Yeah . . .

*BK*: Why would your mother say courage, do you think, Anna?

*Anna*: I don't know . . .

*BK*: How do . . . how do you understand that word? . . . What does it mean?

*Anna*: (*searchingly*) . . . I don't know . . .

*Maria*: (*laughs*) . . . It is like when you have like, you think something is possible and doing it . . . so you go and do it because things can't work out . . . so like I think my mum would want us to get courage, because it is like, not many people . . . if some day I got married and I had my own kids and my husband left me and then got married to some other person, I would never look after the children . . . I would like look after the children but I would not like take care of them for the rest of my life, because . . . I think that the courage like she has is really like strong . . .

*BK*: What do you think, Anna, about courage? that word?

*Anna*: I think she knew she was going to die and if she, like, she had to pick someone, if she knew Isabella yeah, and she had to pick someone like for us to live with, someone to take care of us she obviously would pick her . . . like they knew each other as friends for example, but even though she would have because she knew that she was going to pass away, she obviously would have told us to have courage because she knew it was not going to be easy for us from then . . . so I think she . . . yeah . . . courage . . . yeah . . .

*BK*: So courage is something which keeps you going?

*Anna*: Yeah . . .

*BK*: So it keeps you going . . . even in the face of such a tragedy . . . that you had in your lives . . . courage keeps you going . . . (*silence for some seconds*) . . . And you are saying somehow Isabella has got it . . .

*Anna*: Yeah. . . .

*BK*: Anything else your mother would say?

*Anna*: She would say . . . work . . .

The session finished soon after this sequence. What began as a general hypothesis about the relationship between mothers/carers and children had become a much more detailed, particular, and contextual picture of the relationship between Anna, Maria, and Isabella, including their relationships with other significant persons such as their dead parents and their half-siblings. By the end of the session, I knew much more about the meanings attributed to these relationships in this family and about the way Anna, Maria, and Isabella individually were connected to these meanings. There were important Brazilian/Portuguese elements in this, but there were also individual and personal issues. In one sense, aiming for "thick description" *is* a process of deconstruction. Attempting to understand something from different points of view means that a theme, an issue, or an idea has to be taken apart, although it can never be completely estranged, in the same way that a print of a photograph always must in some way reflect its negative. Or, turning this on its head, as White (1992) has quoted Geertz (1986) again quoting someone else, namely Trilling: "it is the copying that originates" (White, 1992, p. 380). The taking apart must be followed by a putting back together so that something else, and perhaps new meanings, emerge; however, although these will be new, they will also always have some relationship to the original theme. This is what is systemic about meaning. Moving towards a conversation about "courage" and the meanings of this idea in this family was a new event, a new process, which took place in the therapy-room, and everyone had a new experience during which understanding deepened. But this took place on the basis of old patterns and old meanings. It is not so much that something was revealed that was there in the first place, but that a transformation took place and during this process old meanings were recuperated and elaborated upon. The putting back together became expressed by the theme of courage, and I used it subsequently both when we talked about the way this family had survived tragedy—how Anna and Maria could mourn the death of their parents—and also when the conversation was focused on how Anna could manage school and how the family could manage the context in which Anna seemed to be in the wrong too often or how Maria could begin to think of herself as someone who can survive losing things and relationships. This again recalls William James's notion of truth: "The truth of an idea is not a stagnant property inherent in it. Truth *happens* to an idea. It *becomes* true, is *made* true by events. Its verity is in fact an event, a process" (quoted in Jackson, 1996, p. 4).

I think that it was because I held the idea of a system in my mind, an idea that denoted a human condition, that Anna,

Maria, and Isabella were left freer to explore their own views and meanings.

What I have tried to show in this chapter, then, is how using an idea of system which denotes general human themes and relationality (and therefore are meaningful) the therapist can generate language loops and questions that allow her to access her clients' views at the same time as facilitating the emergence of other and different views. The questions did not come out of nowhere but were generated by my systemic view of humanity. This is perhaps what Cecchin and his colleagues are getting at when they find it difficult to distinguish between therapy and research (Cecchin et al., 1992): "The clinician is always watching what the effects of his actions are on the client, and comparing them with what he already knows. Therefore in one sense, his actions and interventions could be called research" (p. 71).

However we refer to this process, it is important to remember that persons always act on the basis of previous experience and with others in mind. It is this connectedness—both to patterns of meaning and to other persons, who may or may not be present—that ethnography as a research methodology aims to understand, and this is also why ethnographic questions are useful in systemic psychotherapy and in particular in any kind of cross-cultural therapy. In order to choose meanings, the therapist needs to understand general human conditions from many particular points of view.

CHAPTER EIGHT

# Choosing meaning: 2

In chapter seven, I showed how the therapist can start from a position that is general enough not to be identified with her own cultural assumptions and yet give some direction to the enquiry and the therapeutic process. The therapist must try to know what she does not know, and this is why she cannot start with a view from nowhere (Nagel, 1986). Indeed, this would be an illusion. I gave some idea of what the "system" that the therapist may want to keep in mind might look like, as well as ethnographic questions and subquestions that can be generated so that the therapist can move towards "thick description". Thick description involves language in the broadest sense, including its expressive use, the experience of participation in the language loop, and, of course, digital and analogic modes of communication (Bateson, 1973). On the basis of these processes, the therapist may, like the ethnographer, be able to access information that is new and, because it may be different from what she expected, needs explaining. But not all this information is also new to the client, because, just like the therapist herself, clients act, think, feel, and exist against the background of previous patterns of interaction and meaning. Information, then, may refer to what Bourdieu (1990) has called doxic experience—that is to say, knowledge that individual persons take for granted and may not be wholly conscious, but is nevertheless imbued with cultural patterns and meaning (see chapter five). This kind of material is a challenge to the therapist because she cannot ask direct questions about it. Nevertheless, her efforts must be directed towards accessing and tuning into these kinds of meanings, and if she is able to do this, she can use it to generate new questions. This requires some clarification, and I shall do this by way of an example.

Together with an Urdu-speaking colleague, I worked with a handsome young Pathan refugee who had arrived in the United Kingdom via Pakistan without knowing much about the whereabouts of his parents. At that time, my colleague was still in training and I was supervising from behind a one-way mirror. The sessions were conducted in Urdu. My colleague, who is also young and beautiful, soon encountered a serious difficulty: the young man became infatuated with her and extremely flirtatious. We discussed this behind the one-way mirror. His behaviour was understandable. He was in great emotional and practical need, and here was someone alone with him in the room who was there to help him. Yet the way he behaved paralysed the young therapist and threatened to lead to another rejecting experience for him. It was a delicate matter, for an exploration of transference with questions like "I wonder what you feel about me, etc." would express a category fallacy (Kleinman, 1987) and would therefore probably be invalid for Pathan ideas about persons and selves. Such an approach would also most likely lead to further entanglement because it would probably become secondary to the process of the interaction that this young man was trying to initiate. After some discussion, my colleague and I decided that she would go into the therapy-room and at the next occasion of flirtatious behaviour she would say quietly to him: "You know you must not treat your *didi* like that." In Urdu, as well as in several other North Indian languages, *didi* means older sister, and in much of Northern India and in Pakistan it is also a term that denotes unmarriageability. That is to say, "*didi*" means a woman of your generation who is older than you and who is connected to you, who cares about you but with whom you cannot have sex and whom you cannot marry. This intervention worked very well, because the young man got the message and yet he did not feel rejected; the therapist also felt more comfortable because she could now put a definite frame on her relationship with her client, one that could be mutually understood.

Obviously, it helped that my colleague and I in different ways knew quite a lot about kinship and marriage structures in the northern part of the Indian subcontinent. This was the system of meanings and relationships in which my colleague herself had been brought up, and I also had personal experience and knowledge from my work as an ethnographer in this geographical area. However, although useful, it was not so much that my colleague and I knew how the kinship terms and meanings that this young man used worked, but that we knew that specific connections and relationships between persons are culturally constructed. This meant, firstly, that we could not assume that for him these were the same as they are for me, a Danish/English or European mental health professional, or for my colleague, a British Pakistani mental health professional. Secondly, it meant that my Pakistani colleague, although of course familiar with the relevant kinship terms and their use, was not automatically able to use the doxic elements of this information, because this part was also doxic information to her. We came up with the intervention by putting our two perspectives together.

The question, then, is what a therapist without this specific prior knowledge might need to know in order to arrive at a train of thought that can address a common human theme—sexual attraction between young men and women—in a culturally sensitive or fitting and therapeutically effective manner—in this case, using the idiom of love and care between brothers and sisters. This can be answered, I think, at two levels. The first level—that specific social relationships always are culturally constructed—is something that contemporary family therapists already accept. The difficulty is how to find ways of working with this when differences between the therapist's own view and that of the clients are wide and only partly conscious. One may argue, however, that it is not wholly valid to use the label of social constructionism until this tricky question is mastered to some degree.

The second level raises the question as a training issue relating to how the first can be properly addressed. The answer of course is this: it is necessary to widen therapists' knowledge of the cross-cultural diversity of human relationships. In the case of the young Pathan man, this second level included my own and my colleague's knowledge and understanding that outside the United Kingdom and the United States kinship is a powerful model both for and of connectedness, and that for some purposes, in many non-European kinship systems persons can be classified as marriageable or unmarriageable. There is no reason why family therapists cannot be exposed to this kind of knowledge, which not only formed the background to our intervention in this case, but which I also use again and again in my cross-cultural work with families to help me generate new questions. But because of this diversity, knowledge cannot be absolute, and the importance of generating questions cannot be underestimated. So, for example, in some kinship systems some women who are classified as sisters are also marriageable—for example, cross-cousins (i.e. the daughters of your mother's brothers or your father's sisters if you are a man: Krause, 1998)—and in all systems there are situations in which persons do not follow rules.

While not all situations will be as clear and striking as this example, much of what goes on in cross-cultural therapy needs addressing at this more covert level and, as the example makes clear, this is a challenge to the therapist. For therapists from cultures and language traditions different from those of their clients, this is obvious; however, even if the background of the therapist is the same as that of the client, this kind of doxic information may not be immediately accessible to either of them. In the rest of this chapter, I give two more examples, both of these from my work with one family, in order to illustrate what kind of information I am talking about and to show how it may be used by the therapist.

## *Self, risk, and uncertainty*

Kirandeep was referred to family therapy by her youngest daughter. This was a few months after Kirandeep had survived a serious suicide attempt which had put her in a coma for several weeks; when she came to therapy, she was still weak and had not fully recovered physically. Kirandeep is a Punjabi Sikh woman in her forties. She had married a Punjabi man in the United Kingdom when she was very young, and the couple had had two daughters: Sarjit who was now 24 years old and Jagdish who was 20. Both daughters were studying at university. While Kirandeep's youngest daughter was a baby, her husband had left her to marry her best friend, with whom he was also expecting a child; a few years before Kirandeep came to therapy he had suddenly died, leaving not only his two daughters but also a son from this second marriage. This had been a personal tragedy with which Kirandeep had bravely struggled and she had managed to bring up her two daughters as well as to study and become a teacher and had worked in a senior position for several years. Her latest suicide attempt had not been her first; she had already taken an overdose on two other occasions, although this attempt had been the most serious one and had been preceded by a period of deep depression.

Kirandeep's unhappiness about the break-up of her marriage had echoed many unhappy memories of her childhood. She was the eldest sister, with two younger sisters and a brother, and although the family were well off she had suffered her mother's emotional neglect and her father's physical abuse. Her mother had died some years back, and her father was now living alone in the family home in the Punjab. Kirandeep's sisters were both married and living in Australia, but the youngest returned frequently to the Punjab and was there fighting for the inheritance, which included the ancestral home as well as land. She had persuaded her father to change the will in her sole favour, overriding previous wills as well as the traditional rights of sons in Northern India to inherit agnatic property. Kirandeep's brother had responded by planning to fight back in the High Court, and a vicious battle between the two sides was on the cards. The brother wanted to enlist Kirandeep on his side and get her to put funds forward for the court case, but he was verbally abusive and insulting towards her; far from feeling that he would be her ally, Kirandeep felt that he too just wanted to use her for his own ends.

I first met Kirandeep and her youngest daughter with my colleague Farra Khan for a couple of sessions, and then I and my colleague met with Kirandeep on her own. The therapy took place over a period of more than a year, and we evolved a pattern in which I saw Kirandeep on my own but, whenever it was possible and felt important, we also met with her daughters, and my co-therapist continued to be involved in some of these meetings. It was Kirandeep's choice that we spoke English rather than Punjabi, but as will become clear this choice of language did not mean that cultural themes and issues were not important. On the contrary, our work with Kirandeep shows how embedded and prevailing such cultural themes can be.

The extract that follows is from the sixth session, in which I and my colleague met with Kirandeep on her own. In the fifth session, we had spoken in detail about Kirandeep's serious suicide attempt, and she had also talked about herself as a "fighting spirit" and her wish to feel "at peace with herself". She had then disclosed another aspect of her problem, namely her recurring shoplifting. Kirandeep explained that she had been prosecuted for shoplifting in the past and given bail, but that she had shoplifted periodically since then and that, despite the great risk, she knew that she shoplifted because she got "a buzz" out of it. We had talked about shoplifting as a coping strategy—albeit a dangerous one—and as a kind of social suicide because of the immense social shame and loss of status involved if Kirandeep should be caught again. In the session that follows, we are pursuing this conversation and "tracking the life of the shoplifting" (White, 1989). This is also both the central cultural issue and the central therapeutic issue. The cultural issue is this: while White's "externalizing" leaves persons with more control over *themselves,* the Ayurvedic and Unani medical views and the Hindu, Sikh, and Muslim religious views of personhood are more ecological—that is to say, they place more emphasis on the *connectedness* between persons and the physical, spiritual, social, and emotional contexts around them (Bhachu, 1996; Cohen, 1998; Krause, 1989; Malik, 1997; Mehta, 1997; Obeyesekere, 1990; Zimmerman, 1987). This is an important difference. The therapeutic issue is this: since it is well known that such an ecological view is expressed in North Indian kinship and attachment (Kurtz, 1992; Obeyesekere, 1990; Östör, Fruzetti, & Barnett, 1982; Roland, 1988) and therefore probably also forms part of Kirandeep's doxic experiences, the use of an externalizing frame may not go far enough to *resolve* her dilemmas. In some way these implicate her connectedness to other persons, in a culturally appropriate way. I and my colleague took this up in the session in the following way:

*BK*: It is not every time you shop that you shoplift? Or is it?

*Kirandeep*: Every time I shop I shoplift, unless I do not go to the shops . . . there have been . . . yeah I think Friday I just went down to the post office and I did not shoplift then . . . because I went to post a letter or something and that is my local post office and I know the people in there and I just feel very mean doing it to them . . . and my chemist . . . I do not do it there because I always go to that chemist . . . and I don't know if I have a relationship with the people then I do not do it. But if I do not have a relationship then it means nothing . . . and I do not feel any moral conscience or pang at all . . .

*BK*: So a relationship stops you ? . . .

*Kirandeep*: . . . (*sighs*) . . . Yeah . . . but I was wondering, you see, whether I do it because I think I feel oh I am just haunted because everything that has happened in the past, because of all the things my sister did to me, my brother did to me, my father did to me and so it is just, I don't know, in a sense I feel it is the luck of the draw, sometimes you win, sometimes you lose and so if I get away with it then I will . . . and so I feel I am due all of it . . . I mean it all does not make much sense because no judge is going to view it like that . . .

*BK*: Well . . . it is risky . . . it is like taking an overdose . . . it is risk, it is risky . . . how do you normally deal with other risks . . . are you insured?

*Kirandeep*: At the moment I am not . . . I can't afford it . . .

*BK*: What about risks in relationships?

*Kirandeep*: I do not take risks in relationships . . .

*BK*: You don't . . . you did not with your husband . . . ?

*Kirandeep*: That was an arranged marriage . . .

*BK*: Even so . . . emotionally . . .

*Kirandeep*: Oh yes, with him I took a lot of risks and it was very hard . . . when you say risks . . . I loved him, I told him. There is only one person I really loved and that was my husband and the others. . . . I have been fond of them and liked them but not loved them . . . but I did take risks with my husband and I was very badly hurt and let down and rejected . . .

*BK*: . . . Hmm. . . . (*long pause*) Do you plan to shoplift today? . . . Are you going shopping today?

*Kirandeep*: I am too tired, emotionally I am exhausted and I got up early and I did not sleep and I have to prepare for the puppy to come and I have got some gardening to do . . . no I don't plan to go today . . . I am too tired, emotionally and physically I am tired . . .

*BK*: I suppose if the pup is the beginning of another coping mechanism . . . if . . . because I am not really convinced that it is . . . I don't know . . . I can see it could be . . . but somehow I am not sure . . . you seem reckless when you talk about your shoplifting . . . but if the pup was the beginning of another coping mechanism how could you build on it? You see I am a sort of superstitious person I am, and I know that I have had this feeling "Oh I do not know whether Kirandeep is going to be here today" and I guess that the sort of course you are painting for us today . . . you know it is, it is worrying . . .

*Kirandeep*: Yesterday when I went to the shops and there were other customers walking around . . . it was terrible because I was getting paranoid about whether I was being followed or whether that person was a store detective or it was another shopper and it created a lot of tension for me . . . and then when I left the store I tell you I was on pins and needles and I thought I was going to be physically sick you know . . . thinking "am I going to be caught or not." . . . I don't think I can cope . . . I don't feel so strong today . . .

*BK*: But what about tomorrow?

*Kirandeep*: (*sighs*) . . . I have got my baby, I have to look after . . .

*BK*: But you are bound to have to go shopping . . .

*Kirandeep*: Yeah . . . I know . . .

*BK*: I was thinking of the stars or I was thinking of an astrologer who kind of maps your progress you know or can map your progress about what is in your future . . . and I was wondering well if the pup is a beginning and you were saying well actually if I have a relationship with a person in the store then I do not do it . . . so something about relationships that prevents you . . . because you are not reckless in relationships, you are a good person in relationships on the whole . . . I was wondering how you could build on it? . . . Because even with the astrologer who maps your progress there is always a line which is a bit about what you can do . . . isn't there? Even if you go to the Ayurvedic doctor or someone like that there is always something you can do . . .

*Kirandeep*: . . . Yes . . .

*BK*: There is always something about how you can look after your constitution, how you can eat the right sort of things, how you can deal with people in the right sort of way . . . you know . . . if you read the horoscope it often says something like you know "stay in today" so even if it is in fate and I am worried about that, there are still things you can do to steer through. . . . What would it be that steered you through? What would it be that you could do that steered you through?

*Kirandeep*: Although in my religion, you know, we believe that your destiny, you know your *kismat*, is mapped out for you but if there is something terrible that is going to happen or it is predicted that something terrible is going to happen you can actually . . . you can actually lessen the impact of it by prayer . . . and . . . maybe that is one thing . . .

*BK*: Do you pray?

*Kirandeep*: I do pray and I do listen to a lot of holy music, but I do not pray as much as I used to because since I was in hospital I find my concentration had gone, but now it is coming back. I also had really got into meditation and I was doing that very well before I went to hospital, but I found that it is only now in the past couple of weeks that I have been able to . . . for very short periods of time to get my thoughts together and be able to meditate . . . that had totally gone, but now it is . . . I am doing it again, but I do not have that degree of concentration which I had which I had actually built on . . . I was really beginning to feel good about it in autumn of last year . . .

*BK*: But then you got depressed?

*Kirandeep*: Yeah . . . I think what I did wrong at that time is that I did stop taking my antidepressants and then I just went down and then totally. . . . I thought I would substitute meditation for antidepressants and it did not work . . . although I was getting into meditation . . . hmm . . . (*sighs*) . . . The other things I was going to tell you and always something I wanted to do is . . . and I am still working towards it is that I love music and I have this harmonium . . . I find that music is something which transports me into another world, it really does, it moves me totally . . .

*BK*: Do you think it will move you off the course . . .

*Kirandeep*: . . . Of shoplifting . . . I think it would . . . with that and the garden and the pup, you know I have got a lot of things that . . . and reading . . . I read quite a bit and I have got some books which I have not even started reading and then I love watching Indian movies and I have got all these video films which I have borrowed from a friend . . . so it is not that I am short of things to do . . . there is a lot I can do . . . and I could . . . yes I could if I put my mind to saying rather than going shopping or shoplifting I am going to see a movie or I am going to practise my harmonium . . . I have to make a conscious effort myself, I have to talk to myself and say it to myself rather than just being caught in this way . . . yes I will still have to go to the shops I will still have to do shopping but I have not always shoplifted and there is no reason why I should not stop again . . .

*BK*: So the astrologer might say to you today . . . that it looks like a dangerous turbulent time ahead especially when you go shopping, but if you keep your mind on the music, on the pup and talk to yourself about what you should do at the time instead you might be able to weather the storm . . .

*Kirandeep*: Yeah . . . the thing is I have not really talked to myself about not doing it . . . it only occurs to me now that I am discussing it with you that I have not sort of said to myself "well I am going to stop and I am going to do different things" . . . I mean . . .

*BK*: Ok . . . that is good . . .

*Farra Khan*: That is different actually to the last time when you were saying you had not decided whether you wanted to stop . . .

Through my tracking of the shoplifting, we learnt that having a relationship stops Kirandeep from shoplifting. Kirandeep herself then connects this to her family relationships, but she also introduces the idea of luck. It is as if she is saying, that, just as with the shoplifting, it is luck what you end up with—caring relationships or abusive relationships, getting away with a theft or not getting away with it. I chose to highlight the experiential side of this, namely the risk that Kirandeep takes and the uncertainty she experiences. I could have pursued the way relationships help her not to shoplift, but since I already realized how many disappointments Kirandeep has suffered in this area, my hunch is that this will not be very useful. Also, I wanted to let her know that I and my co-therapist shared the experience of uncertainty because of our relationship to her. The shoplifting threatened to terminate the therapy, and this mattered to us. This was a way of sharing our common experience.

Now, risk and uncertainty are doxic themes that are culturally constructed or at least are greatly influenced by cultural orientation (Douglas, 1992), so our uncertainty had to be joined with one that was to some extent isomorphic with Kirandeep's own. We could not just ask her "What is your idea of risk and uncertainty?" to access this material. This is why I started somewhat clumsily by saying that I am a superstitious person. Later on, when I was more sure about Kirandeep's response, I was more confident and able to elaborate on this by mentioning the astrologer and the Ayurvedic practitioner. Then I asked about the "course" on which Kirandeep seemed to be set and what she could do to influence it. One might call this an externalizing frame, but I was carefully balancing this between personal agency on the one hand and external bigger (social) forces on the other. After all, just like some of the philosophers who argued about the Azande (chapter six), I also feel that luck has some influence over my life. Kirandeep responded to this by referring to *kismat,* which means "fate", "fortune", or "destiny" (Singh, 1955). However, at the same time she picked up my suggestion, and at the end we all realized that something had changed since the last session because "talking to herself" appeared as a real possibility.

I want to make two other comments about this sequence. One is that in my clumsy opening about being superstitious I was initiating a new language loop which might have fallen flat. I could have created havoc and upset because I referred to beliefs, which at that point I could not be sure about, as superstition. However, I already knew Kirandeep quite well, and somehow this word seemed acceptable. Even so, I remember feeling uncomfortable after having uttered it. As it turned out, the fit was good enough for us to move on. The other is that in this sequence "the system" that I and my co-therapist kept in mind is of a different order from that referred to in chapter seven as "human conditions", "connectedness", and "relationality". The notion used here is not so generic and not so general. It refers, rather, to doxic, culturally constructed experiences and knowledge, embedded and implicated in what persons think, feel, and do. This system is a particular social system—in this case, loosely defined (remember, social systems can only be defined loosely) as made up of relationships between people who refer to themselves as Punjabi or Sikh in some way, be it in terms of ancestry, language, or ideas about how to do some things—and, as I discussed in part I of this book, it deeply implicates local meanings and culture.

### *Kinship relationships, substance, and status*

As I have mentioned, Kirandeep had an arranged marriage to a Punjabi man in England when she was very young. She had up till then been more or less completely under her mother's control, and when she came to England she and her husband first lived with her husband's parents. Her sister-in-law—her husband's sister—was also living nearby and she saw her often. Traditionally in North India, this kind of situation is one that may be tense and difficult for a new daughter-in-law. A woman has rights in both her own family and in her husband's family but there may be conflicts of loyalty, and it also takes time before a young woman can establish herself *vis-à-vis* her in-laws. In English and Danish families, tensions between parents and the partners of their children and the parents of these partners is also not unknown (Simpson, 1998), but in North India these articulate particular cultural themes. These themes include the importance of kinship groups and the idea that persons should marry within their own caste or status group, even though within social groups there may still be pressures to find the most prestigious connections for your children and for yourself. These themes are also expressed in certain etiquettes so that, for example, from a person's point of view there is a difference between the way one may behave towards and address one's own family as opposed to family of one's spouse. Yet, in-laws are important relatives, particularly for women (Östör et al., 1982; Parry, 1979; Raheja & Gold, 1994). In this setting, a most tangible evidence that a person has claims within a system of relationships is expressed in the extent to which a person may have rights to property and land. It is as if the sharing of physical or bodily substances between parents and children is articulated in the way they also share material substances (land, livestock, gold, money) both by using them but also by having rights of ownership in them (Bhachu, 1985; Krause, 1988; Strathern, 1999). Again, this idea is not completely strange to Americans or Europeans, and much family conflict arises over inheritance in English families as well as in Danish families. But it is important not to lose sight of the differences. In Northern India, among Sikhs and Hindus it is as if there is recognition that land and property and other things such as *prasad* (sacred food, a mixture of ghee, honey or sugar, and flour) have, despite being things, a certain subjectivity because this is what has been bestowed on these items by persons and by their relationships either to each other or to God (Gell, 1998; Strathern, 1999). So it is not quite right to say that land may symbolize a kinship relationship; rather, a thing—and in this case land and property—may itself be imbued with agency because "it does not matter, in ascribing 'social agent' status, what a thing (or a person) 'is' in itself; what matters is where it stands in a network of social relations" (Gell, 1998, p. 123). And this will be the case in all societies, but in some this may be recognized more or less explicitly and hence find elaboration in cultural themes.

Against this general description, Kirandeep's situation *vis-à-vis* both her own family and her husband's family is a reversal. It was precisely because of the traditional importance of the agnatic line and of the right of a son to his father's property that Kirandeep's sister's attempts to annul her brother's rights to inherit were so shocking. Annulling Kirandeep's own rights that she had to her family's property according to modern Indian law also threatened to annul her connection to her own family. As a wife she had rights in her husband's property, particularly because she had given birth to children, but the divorce between Kirandeep and her husband had created ambiguity for her. Her daughters were agnates of their father's line and due to inherit a share of their father's property, but there had not yet been a settlement of their father's property. In this way, Kirandeep's position *vis-à-vis* her sister-in-law was ambiguous. In fact, Kirandeep herself considered that her husband's sister was not to be trusted, and, in part, Sarjit and Jagdish blamed this relationship for their mother's depressions and suicide attempts.

Sarjit and Jagdish also had their own conflicts with their mother. These focused on issues of how to live together in the house, with regard to chores such as cleaning, cooking, and washing up. At times these conflicts could get very intense, and on one occasion Kirandeep had left the house and gone to stay overnight with her sister-in-law. My next extract comes from a session with Kirandeep and her two daughters a few weeks after this incident. This session was part of a sequence of sessions that addressed the conflict and disagreements between Kirandeep and her daughters, and Sarjit began by saying that she had been depressed after the last session.

*BK*: (*to Jagdish*) What do you think Sarjit felt despondent about, particularly . . . ?

*Jagdish*: Last week I think that it was some of the things mum was saying about our general behaviour or disrespectfulness . . . and those kind of things, so . . . I think remember asking you? . . .

*Sarjit*: Yeah . . .

*Jagdish*: It did bother me but it did not upset me for the whole day . . . in the same sort of way . . .

*BK*: Hmm. . . . Why would she find that so upsetting? . . .

*Jagdish*: Because I think we both feel that we make an effort to be anything but disrespectful . . . and when it gets brought up in sessions and things do get exaggerated about how little we do and how messy we are . . . it makes what you do seem a bit pointless sometimes . . .

*BK*: Do you think she is still despondent about that . . .

*Jagdish*: Hmm . . . yeah . . . I do not think she is upset about it in the same way and I do not think she is depressed about it in the same way that she was last week . . . but . . . because they are big issues . . .

*BK*: Do you agree with what Jagdish is saying about you?

*Sarjit*: Hmm. . . . Yes . . .

*BK*: So there is sense in which that has not had . . . or even come close to any resolution . . . it is the same kind of situation . . .

*Sarjit*: I think we hit on a lot of timeless problems that we have basically

*BK*: Hmm. . . .

*Sarjit*: . . . and it is a whole thing that I think mum has heard our side of it before and we have heard mum's side of it before, but it does not change that conflict from happening . . . and it is pretty much around those themes that household arguments always . . .

This outlined the issue of conflict between Kirandeep and her two daughters, and in what followed I and my co-therapist enquired about the conflict. I asked about Kirandeep's in-laws—that is to say Sarjit's and Jagdish's *phua* [father's sister] and *chacha* [father's younger brother]:

*BK*: Hmm . . . what about the other issue, about your other relatives about your *phua* and your *chacha*, what about that, because that is something we have heard about almost since you and Kirandeep came to begin with . . . and that is a strange thing that somehow could produce a rift between you but also has a sort of theme running through it because it goes back to your dad and it goes back to families before that and so on . . . and so on . . . what about that?

*Jagdish*: I remember feeling very angry in that first session, but that is quite a while ago with regards to that anyway . . . now I have not seen them, well . . . since mum was in hospital? . . . July . . . something like that . . . and now I don't feel as angry . . . I think I can if I sit down and think about it and on and off . . . but I don't really have the energy to think about it . . .

*BK*: So is it ok for Kirandeep, . . . you think it is ok for you? I mean not that you will decide about these things . . . she will . . .

*Jagdish*: It still bothers me . . .

*BK*: You are still bothered . . .

*Jagdish*: Yeah . . . it still bothers me because of the history of mum's relationship with them, and just the manner in which I witnessed them talking not only about mum but just generally about people in a very dismissive way which I do not like and I do not like the thought of them doing that . . . but at the same time I know that she is going out more than she used to . . . she goes out to see movies and stuff like that but at the same time those people have very much got her down in the past . . . so . . . I think she is happy to go out and see these films but at the same times she comes back and she says "I do not really feel the same about these people any more, they bore me" . . .

*BK*: Do you think she could tell herself when they are . . . I mean you know we all have relationships with lots of people, some, you know, we are very close to, others we do certain things with but we would not do other things and some we do not trust, but we can still spend some time with them . . . do you think that your mum would, kind of, be able to decide for herself when it would be dangerous? and when it is ok to go out with these people who she clearly at some level enjoys seeing ?

*Jagdish*: Hmm. . . . I would say yeah, yeah possibly, because I think at the moment I do not see mum getting . . . she is not spending a huge amount of time and she is very much doing her own thing at the same time. I do not see her getting very attached . . .

*BK*: What do you think Sarjit?

*Sarjit*: I think . . . you know . . . that Indian way of looking at marriage and in-laws, you know, I think that mum very much sees them as family and I think that she would pretty much put all her trust in them if push came to shove. If you ask her she will say "they have been there for me I could not have brought . . ." I mean she brought us up herself, but she would also say that she could not have done this without them, which I think is rubbish. I think she puts a lot of faith in them still, you know . . . she knows what they are like completely, but she won't really admit it, I don't think. I think, even like she will go as far as get herself into a position where she can easily get hurt again even though she knows . . .

*BK*: But she . . . your mother has had some bad experiences in this area hasn't she? . . . of family letting her down . . . not just her in-laws?

*Sarjit*: I think she would not give her family in India as much leeway perhaps, I don't know if they have done like worse things or because they are your blood relatives so you do have higher standards for them. I think she is much more realistic about her family in India . . . she is like, "right I am not going to go and visit them they are just going to cause me grief" which I think is great, she just needs to have a holiday . . .

*BK*: Hmm . . .

*Sarjit*: But I think that about her in-laws it is a bit more fuzzy boundaried . . .

*BK*: Hmm . . . do you think that this comes from . . . I mean you just hinted that this is the way she was brought up, she cannot help it, this is part of a cultural pattern and that is what she is slotting into?

*Sarjit*: Well, partly . . .

*BK*: Or is there something else?

*Sarjit*: I guess they are like . . . her support in that work . . . whether realistic or not they are . . . like . . . who mum has on an adult level . . . that is her peer group if you like, but with that family sort of thing over it, so I guess it is quite a difficult thing to let go and to say "right I am just going to strike out on my own".

*Jagdish*: But she has done that in the past . . .

*Sarjit*: . . . and been totally unhappy when it has been like that . . .

*Jagdish*: Hmm . . .

*Sarjit*: But then they are likely to let her down again . . . so . . .

*FK*: Do you think that has got anything to do with your mum's sense of judgement, kind of her better sense of judgement, because she has been through things with them, they have not got her down yet . . . she continues. I don't know whether she continues the right way, but she maintains her relationship with them and she respects them?

*Sarjit*: I don't know I think that mum is just sweeter-natured than those people are, at the end of the day. I think that she does have a nasty temper and she can blow up but she is not, you know, deliberately spiteful or goes around talking about people in a vindictive way or does not play any sort of weird games with people. You know, yeah if she is angry you know she is angry with you in a very straight up, . . . it is not kind of like backbiting and this kind of playing people off against each other. So I think it is just this sort of difference . . .

*BK*: You know Kirandeep that I think . . . I think, I don't know what Farra thinks and I don't know what your girls think . . . but I think that in one sense one has to choose who one wants to be with and what one wants to do, but that does not mean that it is bad thing to think about why one is choosing to do certain things in life . . . you know sometimes it helps if one looks at or tries to understand why one is doing certain things. I was wondering is Sarjit right, because I . . . it may be my imagination but I sort of heard her saying that you are being . . . you continue to be a good bride . . . in connecting with your in-laws . . . or is there something else to think about in relation to that connection which clearly is important to you?

*Kirandeep*: I must say yes, there is a cultural attachment, but they have been there for me and they are supportive of me and ok they are my in-laws and I do get something from them, it is not just a total one-way street. And I also believe you know

> that, you know there is saying if your arm gets rotten rather than allow the rest of your body to be diseased then it is best to cut off that arm straight away . . . and I think I feel a little bit like that about my own family . . . maybe there are limits to the amount of abuse I will take and I will not go back for more and more abuse if I knew that this is what is going to happen again, so I really think . . . yes I think that they are very right . . . I mean . . . I have been very, very hurt and upset by Kamaljit especially, she definitely has hurt me very severely, and in fact I don't know . . . I was quite attached to my mother-in-law and then Kamaljit became a sort of substitute mother for me you see she mothered me quite a bit and then she is the type that can mean so much and you become so friendly with her and then suddenly she will take the carpet from under your feet and you fall and that is what has happened to me . . . but I guess that has been a learning experience for me—I have matured and I don't expect, I am not that emotionally dependent upon her, but I must say that I am not totally totally strong and independent . . . so I am sort of at a point where I see them, I do not want to see them too much . . .

Here Kirandeep, Sarjit and Jagdish are describing the particular way in which some of the well-known North Indian themes I referred to above are articulated through Kirandeep's feelings, actions, and orientations towards her in-laws. They are talking about how she is affected by these tensions. I chose to highlight this by using the word "bride" to describe Kirandeep now. In English law or in the way these issues are perceived in English society generally, Kirandeep was not of course any longer a bride, but I had a hunch that part of her still felt like a bride or wanted to feel like a bride, and in some way a Punjabi part of her was still in an affinal relationship to her husband's relatives and that she felt she had a claim to be considered this way. Emotionally, she had good reason not only because this is traditionally where a wife belongs in terms of group affiliation, but also because of the disastrous situation in her own family. I chose to use the term "bride" rather than "daughter-in-law" partly because it is at the point when a young woman becomes a bride that her status changes, and partly because the term "bride" is more evocative of the imagery of marriage than the term "daughter-in-law". I could also have used the Punjabi term for daughter-in-law, *nunh*, or bride, *larhi*.

I also chose to refer to marriage in this way because I wanted to denote the more or less doxic themes that underscored Kirandeep's present position and the conflicts she experienced. I think that it was this doxic material that she responded to when she herself went on to describe her own family as a rotten arm, making a direct connection between family relationships and bodily substances. Bringing the doxic material to the fore also helped emphasize the side of Kirandeep that is difficult to integrate into her present family life, namely her past in a different cultural context to that of Sarjit and Jagdish. However, Kirandeep's past contains not only Punjabi cultural material but also physical and emotional abuse, and these two strands are mixed up with each other to such an extent that it is difficult to separate them absolutely. This is taken up by Kirandeep towards the end of the session:

> *Kirandeep*: But what is interesting is that you know when I came here . . . the things my husband said to me, this was earlier on when he would go to Marks and Spencer's to buy clothes and I had no confidence . . . I did not know which nightie to buy or which whatever type, I kept asking him . . . he says "well if you like it buy it" you know . . . and I mean I think that was one of the good things he did say to me . . . he said "don't expect me to be your mother". I mean I felt a bit hurt but it did give me the confidence to say "yes I will just go and buy it" you know, I don't have to get her approval or his approval or whatever . . . and I used to think about my girls that I do not want them to be in the situation, although I find some of the things that they do very annoying, but in a way I am still very proud of them, because I feel that at least they are not like me like I was at sixteen, seventeen or eighteen or twenty, whatever is right and wrong at least they have the confidence to make decisions for themselves . . .
>
> *BK*: You do not want them to be obedient the way you were?
>
> *Kirandeep*: No . . . I would not want them to be the way I was towards my mother . . . no and if I wanted to control them I

think I probably would have started doing a very good job of it and then kept them under my thumb so that they needed my approval for everything . . . and yet I see some girls now and adults who are still going running to their mother to ask . . . and yet I know they both can go and do their things and . . . it makes me feel really good and proud . . .

*BK*: So what do you make of that . . . that your mother does not want you to be obedient?

*Sarjit*: I know what mum means . . . and I think that on the whole that is true, like a majority of the time, but at the same time I think that what your mum did to you and stuff kind of had any effect . . . and your ideas of what parenting and kids and the whole like parent/kids relationship stuff is, does have some of that India stuff in it, cultural stuff and from your family . . . and I think that maybe it is just like a little backlash sometime, like a little side channel, you know what I mean. On the whole I think that what mum is saying is totally true, but maybe that is why it is something that always happens in tense situations when it is kind of like awkward and . . . it is like not instinctual, but it is kind of a reaction . . . like I am the parent here . . .

*BK*: Do you mean that you might interpret that little side lash as being part of mum's story of her mum and India?

*Sarjit*: Yeah, yeah . . . and I think that consciously she has definitely made loads of effort like she is always saying "my mum was opening my mail and I would never want to do that" and she totally never does, so I think that when she thinks about it then definitely it is like totally different, but then there are these occasions when . . . it is kind of a bit of a different story, like she saying that she would hate us to be the way she was with her mother and she loves how independent we are, but then there is also well, I would never speak to my mother the way you spoke to me and you should be like you know respect me in all ways or whatever, or that kind of other side of it . . . so . . .

*BK*: What do you think Jagdish?

*Jagdish*: I agree with Sarjit . . . she is right . . .

Generally speaking the "backlash" or the "side channel" that Sarjit refers to is the doxic experiences in which both Kirandeep's cultural and abusive past are implicated. I thought that this was also from a different point of view what the term "bride" articulated: the particular rights of an Indian bride *vis-à-vis* her own family and her in-laws, and therefore Kirandeep's cultural past and the painful fact that in her case this traditional situation had been reversed much to her detriment. The session finished with positively connoting Kirandeep's attempts to keep some of her cultural heritage as well as her efforts to do things differently for her daughters from how her mother had done things for her (Byng-Hall, 1995). The use of the word "bride" and Kirandeep's reaction to this denoted a moment in which information and experience came together and the patterns particular to this family became clearer. This involved the use of cultural themes that, although reminiscent of my own, also carried particular local (personal and cultural) meanings, and, as in the example of the young Pathan, I and my co-therapist had to keep a particular social and cultural system in mind. We could do this because we already had different types of general knowledge about similar cultures and societies. In the Appendix, I suggest an approach and an exercise than can help therapists move forward when they do not start out with such knowledge. First, in the final chapter I summarize the issues implicated in working with families cross-culturally.

CHAPTER NINE

# From Macpherson to ethnography

In this final chapter, I offer an overview of the processes described in this book. This may be seen as an introduction to the exercise that I outline in the Appendix which therapists and other health professionals can use either by themselves or in teams when they feel stuck over cross-cultural issues, be this in therapy or in organizational dynamics.

I have implied that just like in any other form of communication, communication in therapy is an uncertain process. No one can ever know the full extent of the patterns and processes that are implicated in and impact on what we do, feel, and think, and in social life it is a matter of fit, of more-or-less patterns rather than rigid rules. These are observations about social life in general, and if they hold for ourselves they also hold for others, regardless of cultural and social background. I have specifically been writing about cross-cultural work, but it follows that no clear boundaries can be drawn between cross-cultural and intra-cultural work. In one sense, therefore, good practice is no less than good cross-cultural practice, and we are therefore also addressing much wider issues of ethics and clinical governance. But we must also be aware that difference of colour and culture is a special case because differences of this nature easily become vehicles for politics, hierarchy, and other social processes, in particular obfuscating ways (Gilroy, 2000; Wallerstein, 2000). This is why the Macpherson Report on the inquiry into the murder of Stephen Lawrence is a milestone in race relations in Britain.

Let me now, therefore, be more specific about the questions raised by the Stephen Lawrence Inquiry and the Macpherson Report in relation to family therapy. We must ask ourselves "hard questions" (Waldergrave, 2000). I have suggested that in the practice of cross-cultural therapy, such questions should address the way we use our own culturally constructed ideas and assumptions about such issues as relationships, risk, causation, personhood, kinship, and rationality (this list is not, of course, exhaustive) as if these assumptions are universally valid for all cultures and societies. We may not be aware, or may be only dimly aware, of many of these assumptions because they seem to us natural and often form the unstated foundation for our professional theories about human health and suffering. But perhaps our most pernicious assumption is to be found in our failure to acknowledge that we make assumptions in the first place. This is "the view from nowhere" (Nagel, 1986), and it may equally be the view of the master conversationalist (Anderson & Goolishian, 1988), the liberator of subjugated knowledges (White & Epston, 1990), the Western psychiatrist, psychologist, or anthropologist (Kirmayer, 1994; Kleinman, 1987; Kleinman & Kleinman, 1996; Littlewood, 1991), or the modern or postmodern psychotherapist. Whether we believe that we start by knowing everything, or that it is possible to start by "not knowing" (Anderson & Goolishian, 1992) or coming to our clients with an "open mind" (Dyche & Zayas, 1995; Falicov, 1998; Laird, 1998) or without presuppositions (Weingarten, 1998, p. 6), in this respect we are in the same boat. As Macpherson and his team pointed out (Macpherson, 1999, p. 31), we must begin by acknowledging that there is a failure.

Make no mistake. I am not arguing that social constructionism did not draw attention to important shortcomings that had been overlooked by positivist paradigms as far as human communication is concerned. It most definitely did do just that. It was an improvement, for example, to realize that truth cannot be observed and that the observer, researcher, or therapist is part of the process in which she herself is participating. However, when it comes to cross-cultural therapy, it is also clear that narrative therapy approaches cannot by themselves solve the problems of power and of how the therapist becomes attuned to diversity. It is as if cross-cultural communication, being a specific instance of a general case, highlights issues about diversity and difference which may not be obvious but nevertheless are present in all communication between persons. From this point of view, the narrative therapist has difficulties because much of the relevant material in therapy is doxic—that is to say, material that persons take for granted—and is therefore not directly available to either client or therapist. This means that access to this type of experience and knowledge is not necessarily straightforward, especially when, as in cross-cultural work, what clients and therapists take for granted may differ significantly.

And even though doxic experiences are unconscious, they are not simply personal or private. Fonagy and his colleagues' revised attachment model (1995) and Smith's language loop (1997) show that patterns of communication between persons, although not rigid, have some continuity over time. The reason for this is that children do not only internalize an image of a carer, as Bowlby thought, but also internalize a reflective process implicated in their relationships with carers (Fonagy et al., 1995). This reflexivity and recursivity is an aspect of all relationships because in any kind of communication agents must more or less accurately anticipate the response if communication is to carry on successfully (Smith, 1997). These patterns of communication therefore implicate relationships, not only represented as the connection between persons, but also as internalized images, constructs, assumptions, or expectations of individuals. Bateson (1973), of course, argued that such patterns are not only about action and behaviour but also always implicate meaning. Doxic material is thus to some extent (to what extent does not concern me here) relational, systemic, and culturally and socially constructed, but it is constructed in this way before the therapy session and through the accumulated processes of communications and relationships which make up a person's life. Until it is addressed, doxic material may thus not feature in the awareness of either therapist or client, although the therapy may provide the context in which it is unknowingly reproduced. In this way, doxic experiences include past experiences and old meanings. Taking this on board means that we need to find a way of accessing the systemic and cultural aspects of the backgrounds against which our clients have lived and continue to live their lives, while at the same time becoming aware of the extent to which we take our own cultural premises for granted. However, since in these respects we are exactly like our clients—that is to say, we are also not aware of all the meanings of what we do, think, and feel—taking a stance of "not knowing" (Anderson & Goolishian, 1992) or "naiveté" (Dyche & Zayas, 1995) or "radical listening" (Weingarten, 1998) or asking that therapists question their own assumptions, or keep an open mind, or try "not to have any meanings" (Andersen, 1992) are all approaches that do not go far enough (Bertrando, 2000; Boscolo & Bertrando, 1996). It is precisely because we are naturally inclined to ignore the fact that doxic experiences are socially and culturally constructed that we need explicit strategies to help us address these issues.

## *What is old, what is new?*

I am an epigenetic therapist (Bertrando, 2000). My views have evolved during the years, and I have been influenced by almost all the major approaches in family therapy, as well as, of course, by my anthropological training before I became a therapist. In this way my therapy is eclectic. I emphasize Bateson's pattern and continuity and especially the idea that meanings are old patterns. With the structuralists I agree that one must join the system, but my joining means joining persons as well as the meanings that persons are trying to communicate. The positive aspects in my approach derive from my view of understanding as attunement rather than as logical consistency and that it is not a stance but a philosophical and a moral orientation. I recognize that many of the decisions about where my therapeutic work is going are mine and that I may have to be strategic in questioning myself and being useful to my clients. I like the idea of curiosity, but I also recognize its limits if only turned on to my clients. I want to convey a notion that is more recursive, which elicits a clearer response from me, the therapist. Perhaps the Danish word *forbløffelse,* which Hastrup (1992) translates as "astonishment" but which also means "amazement", conveys something of what I am getting at. Hastrup uses this term to describe ethnography. Astonishment or amazement is something that you feel in your body and therefore may become the first step towards discovering something new about yourself and about the situation. The next step can be disapproval or it can be reflection. While we may at some stage disapprove, it is an aspect of our professionalism that we first aim to make it possible for ourselves to reflect.

In a general sense, the process of therapy is a Euro-American mode of reflection. Other people may tell a myth or a story or enact a ritual, and these methods may implicate entirely different assumptions regarding social relations, personhood, and agency (Briggs, 1996; Howe, 2000; Lewis, 1980; Laderman & Roseman, 1996; Schieffelin, 1996). While reflection is a human ability, it is also articulated in different, culturally constructed ways. For example, the Just Therapy team's use of caucuses (groups of categories of persons going away to reflect) is also a Samoan process of social communication, and reaching consensus (Tamasese, Tuhaka, & Waldergrave, 2000), and Andersen (1992) was influenced by the Sami way of listening to suffering and bereavement. I therefore emphasize reflection as a way of confronting myself and making clear to myself what I know as a way of moving towards asking questions about what I do not know, rather than, as Tom Andersen (1992) describes as the process in reflecting teams, "a shifting back and forth between talking and listening" (p. 62). I would call Andersen's reflecting teams a language loop and I think that this comes after reflection. The kind of reflecting I am talking about then is done by persons, but it can be done by persons in groups, indeed it is something with which we can help each other. And of course in a cross-cultural situation one place to start might be to reflect about reflecting, since we cannot assume that this is a process that takes place in a similar manner in different cultural contexts. But neither reflecting about reflecting nor talking about talking can be approached from a position of no meanings; it can only be approached with the intention of confronting what my own meanings are. And this is where my freedom to explore other meanings begins. This is why therapists must learn how to talk to a particular client or family just as I have argued they must learn how to ask (Krause, 1998). My idea of reflection thus has something in common with the idea put forward by Haber (1994) when he talks about response-ability and the therapist as his own co-consultant, but it is also a response to Cooklin's (1994) challenge to develop the professionalism of reflection in order to "protect our clients from our own self-indulgence" (p. 290).

## *Different levels of "system"*

I have suggested that one legacy from social constructionism in family therapy thinking is that the idea of the cybernetic system has been replaced by the idea of the social system. This move has taken place alongside a general debate about the social construction of illness and suffering (Hacking, 1995, 1998, 1999; Littlewood, 1998; Young, 1995) and also alongside the increasing importance of feminist studies and scholarship (Segal, 2000). From this point of view, it is a mistake to consider the narrative school of therapy as in some way an alternative to systemic therapy, for, as I have shown, narrative therapists also use the idea of a social system to generate questions and conversation in the therapy-room. What is different is that the narrative therapist may not be explicit about the fact that this is what she is doing, and it is perhaps not difficult to understand her reluctance.

A cybernetic system has rules, regularity, and predictability. A social system, however, is different. First, it is much more difficult to decide who belongs and who does not belong to a social system. For some purposes some persons may be inside, and for other purposes the same persons may be outside. A social system has no clear boundaries, and persons usually belong to many social systems. It makes a difference (and sometimes a very big difference) to those inside it that they are classified in this way (Hacking, 1999). Second, because the agents in social systems are persons who react and are able to reflect on these reactions in a variety of different ways, the patterns in social systems are "more-or-less" patterns and routines rather than predictable repetitions. Persons must more or less understand each other in order to communicate, they must more or less anticipate the response of others, and they must more or less agree on ideas about how things should be done, but there is still room for uncertainty and different interpretations and meanings. Third, because these processes and these relationships constitute social systems, social systems have no inherent objective other than that which persons who participate in them might give them, and this, as we know, is largely socially constructed and culturally articulated. For these reasons, and perhaps there are others too, the *social* system is—as is culture, which it implicates—a difficult and complex concept. It associates predictability with uncertainty, closure with possibility, the past with the present and the future, and restraint with choice.

Given the traditional emphasis in family therapy on what goes on in the therapy-room, on the future, and on making choices and facilitating change, it is perhaps not surprising that the demise of the cybernetic systems model heralded theoretical caution for some family therapists. Perhaps this is why a preference came about for engaging with the most obvious and most explicit aspects of social construction in the therapeutic process—that is to say, the way therapists and clients construct together. However, as I have noted, this obscures important processes and material; in particular, it obscures the way diversity and difference implicate pattern and continuity, and it is this which is highlighted in cross-cultural work. The therapist therefore needs a less cautious approach, one that allows her to be more confident as well as to take more risks. I suggest that the idea of "system" can assist the therapist with this in three ways or on three levels.

The first of these is by acknowledging that when we refer to system as social system, we are also acknowledging that we cannot easily make judgements about rationality or irrationality. This does not mean that clients always make sense, for persons in any culture or social system may be confused, deluded, badly informed, or of contradictory dispositions. It means that what persons say, feel, and think must be understood initially from the point of view of the cultural and social context in which these events take place. This is not, of course, new to family therapists, for connectedness is a cornerstone of a systemic approach. However, cross-cultural work also demands that, while this connectedness is being kept in mind, the reasons for it and the meaning of it are not being prejudged. I discussed this in chapter six, where I warned against confusing relationality with rationality.

Second, I have used the idea of "system" as a generic model that refers to "the human condition"—that is to say, more broadly to fundamental aspects of humanness. These include connectedness between persons in social relationships, the recursive nature of communication processes, attachment, suffering, agency, embodiment, personal transformation through physical growth, birth, death, bereavement, language, and meaning-making. The model, which I call System 1, implies that there are a limited number of ways of being human (Kirmayer, 1994; Kleinman & Kleinman, 1996). I use this model as a kind of hypothesis and as a guide to general statements that allow me to ask questions about the way these general human issues are experienced and negotiated in particular families. In chapter seven, I referred to these questions as ethnographic questions, and I use them not only to join with families and clients but also to join with and attune to their meanings. This becomes my experience of a particular family, but it is only gradually as I am able to put together a description from many points of view—a "thick description", to use Ryle's phrase—that I am able to choose which of the meanings seem to fit.

The third level, System 2, follows from this. Here, the system refers to the social and cultural patterns of meaning, thoughts, and action which are the contexts in which clients live and to these contexts as experienced by clients in the past. It is this that some people may prefer to call culture. This idea of "system" is more specific and local, and I referred to this in chapter eight where I also noted that this system includes experiences and even patterns of which clients may be unaware or may take for granted. Here, I used information that either has been acquired through earlier phases of therapy, using System 1, or has been acquired through my own experiences or exposure to cultural diversity. I noted that, while cultural knowledge may be useful for the use of "system" at this level because some of this knowledge is doxic, prior cultural experience does not by itself guarantee success. As I described, using System 2 involves introducing ideas that may be implicit but have not been discussed, and therefore it is this level in particular that involves the therapist taking risks. While using both System 1 and System 2 involves entering the language loop, it is in using System 2 that the "fit" in the language loop is seriously being put to the test.

Thus, while cross-cultural therapy requires a systemic approach, it also presents a challenge to family therapy. This is the challenge of a paradigmatic shift to a model of practice that, while addressing the systemic nature of human connectedness, is also able to address patterns as more-or-less patterns rather than rigid repetitions. It is the more-or-less aspects that gives the cross-culturally practising therapist freedom to venture into language loops with persons and families from cultural and ethnic backgrounds different from her own. But to safeguard this freedom, she must also take responsibility for asking questions that, like ethnographic questions, are valid and attuned to her clients' points of view, and one way of doing this is to reflect about her own actions, feelings, thoughts, and participation. In this way, the therapist may acquire understanding of the assumptions of others by first acknowledging her own.

# *APPENDIX: THE REFLECTIVE LOOP*

## *About the reflective loop*

Because there is no perfect fit in communication and because there is even less fit in cross-cultural communication, therapists who work cross-culturally must sometimes take great risks. Taking risks means that mistakes will be made, and therapists therefore also need to be able to get unstuck in ways that are respectful and do not lead to further discrimination. The "reflective loop" is an exercise that can be used to minimize discrimination. In it, I adopt the language loop (Smith, 1997) to a process that begins as self-reflection and moves on to questions that aim to be open, respectful, and curious and are likely to lead to new experiences for clients and therapists and, eventually, to a dialogue (or a language loop in the way used by Smith that, in turn, will call for further self-reflection by the therapist, new open questions, and new dialogues. I also follow Hildebrand (1998) in assuming that experiential learning is the most comprehensive way to learn. As an exercise, the reflective loop is therefore not aimed at how therapists can give up their own models and ideas in a simplistic way or at how they can adopt foreign ideas as a kind of idealization of "the other". Rather, it is aimed at how therapists can develop ways of thinking about their own ideas and conceptions as only one possible way in which things can be done. By these means, it is aimed at enhancing sensitivity to cultural and ethnic differences.

The reflective loop involves two kinds of questions: self-reflective questions, and the kinds of questions that I have described as open and likely to lead to new experiences. The second kind of questions I have referred to as ethnographic questions in the previous pages of this book (see chapter seven); since I propose that systemic psychotherapists should learn to ask ethnographic questions, a brief outline of ethnography is in order at this point.

Ethnography is a research method used in anthropology during fieldwork. Ethnography aims to capture detail, and it is therefore more similar to annotation (Schieffelin, 1996) than it is to a flowing narrative or the plot of a story. Doing fieldwork and collecting ethnographic details involve a complex set of activities: listening to speech in action, learning how to ask, learning how to talk, having conversations, conducting interviews, asking for specific pieces of information, observing behaviour, gossiping, and participating in activities. This is why the method of ethnography is often described summarily as participant observation, and linguistic competence is a tool towards this end rather than an end in itself (Krause, 1998). But ethnography is not just about being there in the sense of "I was there and I know it is true"; it is also about approaching one's own observation and participation in a disciplined way.

An ethnographic account is one that supports the claims it makes. It is descriptive and explanatory, but not predictive (Davies, 1999). The aim is to enhance validity. This was a point made by Arthur Kleinman, a cross-cultural psychiatrist. Kleinman (1987) argued that in order for cross-cultural psychiatric research to be methodologically sound, researchers must avoid category fallacies—that is to say, they must avoid asking questions using categories and ideas that are not valid or do not have meaning for the research subjects. Research questionnaires and schedules derived from Western psychiatry, for example, are not necessarily valid for populations from non-Western cultures. The questions must be asked in a way that makes sense to those who are going to give the answers. Kleinman was referring to the vast body of cross-cultural research that has taken place in psychiatry, but his argument also applies to both clinical work and research in family therapy. So, for example, it is well known that classical attachment theory and the Adult Attachment Interview reflect a Euro-American view of relationships. It will not do therefore to ask questions of Puerto Rican mothers (Harwood, Miller, & Irizarry, 1995), Gusii mothers (LeVine et al., 1994), Tamil mothers (Trawick, 1992), or Kpelle mothers (Lancy, 1996) without taking note of, for example, cultural variation in the recognition of different emotions, in ideas about child development, and in ideas about culturally preferred behaviour and differences in patterns of kinship organization. The questions and communications initiated by family therapists must also be "experience-near" rather than "experience-far" (Geertz, 1974; Kohut, 1971), and the reflective loop is a tool that can help therapists do this.

The reflective loop exercise can be used in different ways. It can be used as a series of steps that therapists can go through by themselves either before a therapy session or when they need to take stock of their own effectiveness. Alternatively, it can be used as an exercise by a group of people, but it is important that the participants can trust each other. If you want to do the exercise as a large group, you should join together in groups of four or five persons; a leader for the whole group could be chosen. The task of the leader is to guide participants through the steps and the feedback and to make sure that each group addresses the same clinical material at each step. It is important that participants remember their examples and their particular difficulties, and this is why it may be helpful to have a leader or a person who focuses on this, although you may find that you can do this collectively. The exercise can be used in this way with trainees, although not, I think, during early stages of training.

## *Using the reflective loop: the exercise*

*STEP 1*

A. Ask yourselves [yourself, if you are on your own] the following questions in relation to specific clinical material from your own work:

  i. where are my difficulties?
  ii. which ideas am I pursuing?
  iii. which professional and lay models am I using?
  iv. how do these fit my own situation?
  v. what assumptions am I making?

B. You are encouraged to keep hold of these questions; if you are in a group, participants should now feed back to each other.

*Comment*: It is important that participants can trust each other with this material, that they draw specific examples from their own practice, and that they remember their examples and their particular difficulties throughout the exercise.

*Professional pointer*: This first step begins with the observation by Macpherson and his team that the problem must be realized before we can do something about it (Macpherson, 1999, p. 31); the question raised, therefore, is: where in your work as family therapists do you find difficulties? It may be difficult to manage addressing the idea of failure directly, but a reference to Macpherson may help, and it is also important to remember that this a strategy. For example, we may not, as the policemen who attended to Stephen Lawrence did, assume that black people cannot be victims, but we do make other assumptions. So what are they? Participants should be able to move beyond "I do this because this is the way it must be done" or "I think this because this is the only way to think about this problem" to "This is the way I think, but it is only one way." Participants need to be curious about some personal or professional idea that they themselves hold about the way something should be done, or the way they themselves and their friends, colleagues, and peers think about it. They should turn curiosity and scrutiny onto themselves.

*Example*: I might consider that mothers, fathers, and carers must talk to and stimulate their children and even that this is a natural way for carers to communicate with their children. Or I might consider that infants and small children have to get used to being on their own—for example, when they go to sleep or for short periods when they play—or that small children are most attached to their own mother. Or I may notice that I am pleased when my own children show others how clever they are.

### *Step 2*

A. On your own or in your groups you should now ask the following questions:
   i. how can I find out about how my clients see these issues without forcing my own culturally constructed assumptions onto them?
   ii. what questions do I need to ask to find how they see this issue?
   iii. what would I answer if I were asked?
   iv. how can I check these issues out?
   v. whom should I ask?
   vi. can I ask directly?

B. Participants should feed back to each other and describe how they arrived at the questions that they feel that they can ask clients.

*Comment.* It is difficult for anyone to go beyond their own assumptions. This seems to be a natural aspect of being human and is not some kind of fault (see chapter one). So, although this step can be done by a therapist by herself, it is helpful to have one or more colleagues together around this task. The key is for participants to encourage each other to be creative and to feed back to each other at the end of this step.

*Professional pointer.* Step 2 is aimed at formulating ethnographic questions or questions that avoid as much as possible the committal of a category fallacy (Kleinman, 1987). This is relatively straightforward if we are talking about issues that are immediately accessible to experience. It is more complex if our questions refer to doxic experiences—that is to say, material about which persons are unaware. In such a case, information must be accessed indirectly. For example, when I wanted to understand the way British Sikhs experience, communicate, and express emotion (Krause, 1989), I could not simply ask: "How do you show that you are upset?" Of course, I could get some answers to this question, but a comprehensive understanding only emerged when I also asked about physical processes in the body, diet, weather, and ideas about good and bad persons. To take another example, when Jacobson-Widding (1997) wanted to find out about how the Shona-speaking Manyika of Zimbabwe think about morality, she could not simply ask about *tsika*, the term that seemed the nearest translation. *Tsika* means the "proper way to greet people", and this term was therefore not equivalent to her own notion of "morality". Hence, she also needed to know what had happened in specific cases involving breaches of morality and the way these were explained. In the case of this exercise, therefore, the more committed and creative participants have been at Step 1 and the more they have been able to question their own assumptions, the more able they will be in developing their curiosity at Step 2.

> *Example.* If we stay with the example of child-rearing and attachment which I used in Step 1, I might, for example, myself remember that the first relationship term my baby uttered was "mum". I can turn this memory into a question about relationship terms used by children or adults in my client's family. What was the first relationship your son could name? Was this just because of your family, or is this the first relative whom children usually name? Did he like this person? Why? Do you like this person? What was the first relationship you could name yourself?—and so on and so on. I could then perhaps move on to the names of relationships in general and the meaning of these names. In a cross-cultural context, this is guaranteed to bring forth a wealth of important information.

This is the end of the exercise if you are doing it in a large group. In a therapy workshop or by yourself, you go on to Step 3.

*Step 3*

A. During the next therapy session, ask the questions you generated at Step 2. You may have found a fit that is good enough for you to enter the "language loop".

B. Use Step 1 and Step 2 in relation to the following events that may occur during the therapy session:

   i. mistakes
   ii. analogic communication (how and not just what is said)
   iii. patterns (in words and actions)
   iv. the telling of a life story
   v. your own reactions to what you hear and see
   vi. co-temporality (the therapy as a social and political event).

*Comments.* In their work, therapists must strive towards a good-enough fit in the communication between themselves and their clients. This "fit" can always be better and can never be perfect. This is what I have referred to as a more-or-less pattern (see chapter four). As a result of these more-or-less patterns, there are always other perspectives and meanings possible. The above list refers to events that may occur in the therapeutic session, and they link the therapeutic dialogue to the wider contexts in which this therapeutic dialogue takes place. These contexts include the present and the pasts of both clients and therapist. Therapists should therefore be encouraged to ask self-reflective and ethnographic questions about these events.

*Professional pointers.* The five types of events listed in Step 3 are familiar to family therapists, although somewhat out of fashion. They all refer in some way to what used to be called "process" in contrast to "content" and to what in family therapy jargon we may denote as "meta-". Although they are not without meaning, the meaning of each of them may not be obvious and may not be easily accessible.

> *Example.* When clients from different cultural and ethnic backgrounds tell us their life stories, we may be able to empathize as human beings (we may draw on what in chapter six I have referred to as System 1) but we will not be able to see the

contexts of their lives without further questions. The more horrific and traumatic our clients' life stories, the more natural our reactions and the more we might be blind to diversity. Certainly, the telling of a life story is an event in the present, but it also refers to events in the past, the background and premises of which may not be clear to us. This is why a particular commitment on the part of the therapist is necessary. No contemporary mental health professional can afford to forget the social and political situation that is the context for the therapeutic encounter between her and her clients from less privileged cultural and ethnic populations. And this, as we have seen, leads back to the Macpherson Report and its recommendation that we must reflect about both conscious and unconscious aspects of our own participation.

# REFERENCES


Andersen, T. (1991). *The Reflecting Team: Dialogues and Dialogues about Dialogues*. New York: W. W. Norton.

Andersen, T. (1992). Reflections on reflecting with families. In: D. McNamee & K. S. Gergen (Eds.), *Therapy as Social Construction*. London: Sage.

Anderson, H. (1997). *Conversation, Language and Possibilities: A Post-modern Approach to Therapy*. New York: Basic Books.

Anderson, H. (1999). Reimagining family therapy: reflections on Minuchin's invisible family. *Journal of Marital and Family Therapy, 25* (1): 1–8.

Anderson, H., & Goolishian, H. (1988). Human systems as linguistic systems: preliminary and evolving ideas about the implications for clinical theory. *Family Process, 27* (4): 371–393.

Anderson, H., & Goolishian, H. (1990). Beyond cybernetics: comments on Atkinson and Heath's "Further Thoughts on Second-order Family Therapy". *Family Process, 29*: 157–163.

Anderson, H., & Goolishian, H. (1992). The client is the expert: a not-knowing approach to therapy. In: S. McNamee & K. Gergen (Eds.), *Therapy as Social Construction*. London: Sage.

Banks, M. (1996). *Ethnicity: Anthropological Constructions.* New York & London: Routledge.

Barth, F. (1969). *Ethnic Groups and Boundaries: The Social Organisation of Culture Difference.* Bergen: Universitets Forlaget; London: George Allen & Unwin.

Bateson, G. (1958). *Naven.* London: Wildwood House.

Bateson, G. (1973). *Steps to an Ecology of Mind.* St Albans: Paladin.

Bateson, G. (1978). Comments to John Weakland. In: M. M. Berger (Ed.), *Beyond the Double Bind.* New York: Brunner/Mazel.

Bateson, G. (1979). *Mind and Nature: A Necessary Unity.* London: Fontana.

Battaglia, D. (1995). Problematizing the self: a thematic introduction. In: D. Battaglia (Ed.), *Rhetorics of Self-Making.* Berkeley, CA: University of California Press.

Benjamin, W. (1936). *Illuminations,* edited by H. Arendt. London: Pimlico, 1999.

Berger, M. M. (1978). *Beyond the Double Bind.* New York: Brunner/Mazel.

Bertrando, P. (2000). Text and context: narrative, postmodernism and cybernetics. *Journal of Family Therapy,* 22 (1): 83–103.

Bhachu, P. (1985). *Twice Migrants: East African Sikh Settlers in Britain.* London & New York: Tavistock.

Bhachu, P. (1996). Identities constructed and reconstructed: representations of Asian women in Britain. In: G. Buijs (Ed.), *Migrant Women: Crossing Boundaries and Changing Identities.* Oxford: Berg.

Bograd, M. (1988). Scapegoating mother in family therapy: re-exploring enmeshment. In: M. Mirkin (Ed.), *The Social and Political Contexts of Family Therapy.* New York: Gardner Press.

Boon, J. A. (1999). *Verging on Extra-Vagance: Anthropology, History, Religion, Literature, Art. . . . Showbiz.* Princeton, NJ: Princeton University Press.

Boscolo, L., & Bertrando, P. (1996). *Systemic Therapy for Individuals.* London: Karnac.

Bourdieu, P. (1990). *The Logic of Practice.* Cambridge: Polity Press.

Bowlby, J. (1969). *Attachment and Loss, Vol. 1.* New York: Basic Books.

Brah, A. (1996). *Cartographies of Diaspora: Contesting Identities.* London & New York: Routledge.

Briggs, C. L. (1996). The meaning of nonsense: the poetics of embodiment and the production of power in Warao healing. In: C. Laderman & M. Roseman (Eds.), *The Performance of Healing*. New York: Routledge.

Bruner, J. (1990). *Acts of Meaning*. Cambridge: Cambridge University Press.

Burck, C., Frosh, S., Strickland-Clark, L., & Morgan, K. (1998). The process of enabling change: a study of therapist's interventions in family therapy. *Journal of Family Therapy, 20* (3): 253–268.

Byng-Hall, J. (1995). *Rewriting Family Scripts: Improvisations and Systems Change*. New York & London: Guilford Press.

Carrithers, M. (1992). *Why Humans Have Culture: Explaining Anthropology and Human Diversity*. Oxford: Oxford University Press.

Cecchin, G. (1987). Hypothesizing, circularity and neutrality revisited: an invitation to curiosity. *Family Process, 26*: 405–415.

Cecchin, G., Lane, G., & Ray, W. A. (1992). *Irreverence: A Strategy for Therapists' Survival*. London: Karnac.

Cohen, L. (1998). *No Aging in India: Alzheimer's, the Bad Family and Other Modern Things*. Berkeley, CA: University of California Press.

Combs, G., & Freedman, J. (1998). Tellings and retellings. *Journal of Marital and Family Therapy, 24* (4): 405–408.

Cooklin, A. (1994). Response to Haber. *Journal of Family Therapy, 16* (3): 285–292.

Csordas, T. J. (1996). Imaginal performance and memory in ritual healing. In: C. Laderman & M. Roseman (Eds.), *The Performance of Healing*. New York & London: Routledge.

Dallos, R. (1997). *Interacting Stories: Narratives, Beliefs and Therapy*. London: Karnac.

Dallos, R., & Urry, A. (1999). Abandoning our parents and grandparents: does social construction mean the end of systemic family therapy? *Journal of Family Therapy, 21* (2): 161–188.

Davies, C. A. (1999). *Reflexive Ethnography: A Guide to Researching Selves and Others*. London & New York: Routledge.

Dell, P. F. (1989). Violence and the systemic view: the problem of power. *Family Process, 28*: 1–14.

DiNicola, V. (1997). *A Stranger in the Family: Culture, Families and Therapy*. New York & London: W. W. Norton.

Douglas, M. (1992). *Risk and Blame: Essays in Cultural Theory*. London: Routledge.

Dwivedi, K. N. (Ed.) (1997). *The Therapeutic Use of Stories.* London & New York: Routledge.

Dwivedi, K. N., & Gardner, D. (1997). Theoretical perspectives and clinical approaches. In: K. N. Dwivedi (Ed.), *The Therapeutic Use of Stories.* London & New York: Routledge.

Dyche, L., & Zayas, L. H. (1995). The value of curiosity and naivety for the cross-cultural psychotherapist. *Family Process, 34*: 389–399.

Eagleton, T. (2000). The estate agent. Review of S. Fish, *The Trouble with Principle. London Review of Books,* 2 March, pp. 10–11.

Evans-Pritchard, E. E. (1937). *Witchcraft, Oracles and Magic among the Azande.* Oxford: Oxford University Press.

Falicov, C. (1998). From rigid borderlines to fertile borderlands: reconfiguring family therapy. *Journal of Marital and Family Therapy, 24* (2): 157–163.

Fonagy, P., Steele, M., Steele, H., Leigh, T., Kennedy, R., Mattoon, G., & Target, M. (1995). Attachment, the reflective self and borderline states. In: S. Goldberg, R. Muir, & J. Kerr (Eds.), *Attachment Theory: Social, Developmental and Clinical Perspectives.* New York: Analytic Press.

Foucault, M. (1973). *The Birth of the Clinic: An Archaeology of Medical Perception.* London: Tavistock.

Foucault, M. (1979). *The History of Sexuality.* London: Allen Lane.

Frosh, S., Burck, C., Strickland-Clark, L., & Morgan, K. (1996). Engaging with change: a process study of family therapy. *Journal of Family Therapy, 18* (2): 141–162.

Fruggeri, L. (2000). Conference address. "The Double Description as a Guideline for Therapy." Marlborough Family Service (11 February).

Geertz, C. (1973). *The Interpretation of Cultures.* London: Fontana Press, 1993.

Geertz, C. (1974). From the native's point of view. *Bulletin of the American Academy of Arts and Sciences, 28* (2).

Geertz, C. (1986). Anti-anti-relativism. *American Anthropologist, 86*: 263–278.

Geertz, C. (1998). William James Lecture, Harvard Divinity School. *Raritan: A Quarterly Review, 18* (3): 1–19.

Gell, A. (1998). *Art and Agency: An Anthropological Theory.* Oxford: Clarendon Press.

Gergen, K. (1994). *Realities and Relationships: Sounding in Social Construction.* Cambridge, MA: Harvard University Press.

Giddens, A. (1984). *The Constitution of Society.* Cambridge: Polity Press.

Gilroy, P. (2000). *Between Camps: Nation, Culture and the Allure of Race.* London: Penguin.

Goldner, V. (1992). Making room for both/and. *Networker* (March/April): 55–61.

Goldner, V., Penn, P., Sheinberg, M., & Walker, G. (1990). Love and violence: gender paradoxes in volatile attachments. *Family Process, 29*: 343–364.

Gower, M. (1999). Back to the future 2. Some millennium thoughts: Don Bloch, John Burnham, Lynn Hoffman, Salvador Minuchin, Rosemary Whiffen, Michael White. *Context, 46* (1): 2–14.

Haber, R. (1994). Response-ability: therapist's "I" and role. *Journal of Family Therapy, 16* (3): 269–284.

Hacking, I. (1995). *Rewriting the Soul: Multiple Personality and the Sciences of Memory.* Princeton, NJ: Princeton University Press.

Hacking, I. (1998). *Mad Travellers: Reflections on the Reality of Transient Mental Illness.* London: Free Association Books.

Hacking, I. (1999). *The Social Construction of What?* Cambridge, MA: Harvard University Press.

Haley, J. (1976). Development of a theory: a history of a research project. In: C. E. Sluzki & D. C. Ranson (Eds.), *Double Bind: The Foundation of the Communicational Approach to the Family.* New York: Grune & Stratton.

Haley, J. (1980). *Leaving Home: The Therapy of Disturbed Young People.* New York: McGraw-Hill.

Harries-Jones, P. (1995). *A Recursive View: Ecological Understanding and Gregory Bateson.* Toronto: University of Toronto Press.

Harwood, R. L., Miller, J. G., & Irizarry, N. L. (1995). *Culture and Attachment: Perceptions of the Child in Context.* New York & London: Guilford Press.

Hastrup, K. (1992). *Det Antropologiske Projekt: Om Forbløffelse.* Copenhagen: Gyldendal.

Henriques, J. (1984). Social psychology and the politics of racism. In: J. Henriques, W. Hollway, C. Urwin, C. Venn, & V. Walkerdine, *Changing the Subject: Psychology, Social Regulation and Subjectivity.* London: Routledge.

Hildebrand, J. (1998). *Bridging the Gap: A Training Module in Personal and Professional Development*. London: Karnac.

Hoffman, L. (1993). *Exchanging Voices: A Collaborative Approach to Family Therapy*. London: Karnac.

Hoffman, L. (1998). Setting aside the model in family therapy. *Journal of Marital and Family Therapy, 24* (2): 145–156.

Horton, R. (1970). African traditional thought and western science. In: R. Wilson (Ed.), *Rationality*. Oxford: Blackwell.

Howe, L. (2000). Risk, ritual and performance. *The Journal of the Royal Anthropological Institute (incorporating Man), 6* (1): 63–80.

Ingold, T. (1986). *Evolution and Social Life*. Cambridge: Cambridge University Press.

Jackson, M. (1996). Introduction: phenomenology, radical empiricism and anthropological critique. In: M. Jackson (Ed.), *Things as They Are: New Directions in Phenomenological Anthropology*. Bloomington, IL, & Indianapolis, IN: Indiana University Press.

Jacobson-Widding, A. (1997). I lied, I farted, I stole. . . . Dignity and morality in African discourse of personhood. In: S. Howell (Ed.), *The Ethnography of Moralities*. London & New York: Routledge.

Jenkins, R. (1992). *Pierre Bourdieu*. London & New York: Routledge.

Jenkins, R. (1997). *Rethinking Ethnicity: Arguments and Explorations*. London: Sage.

Kirmayer, L. J. (1993). Healing and the invention of metaphor. *Culture, Medicine & Psychiatry, 17*: 161–195.

Kirmayer, L. J. (1994). Improvisation and authority in illness meaning. *Culture Medicine & Psychiatry, 18*: 183–214.

Kleinman, A. (1987). Anthropology and psychiatry: the role of culture in cross-cultural research on illness. *British Journal of Psychiatry, 151*: 447–454.

Kleinman, A., & Kleinman, J. (1996). Suffering and its professional transformation: toward an ethnography of interpersonal experience. In: M. Jackson (Ed.), *Things as They Are: New Directions in Phenomenological Anthropology*. Bloomington, IL, & Indianapolis, IN: Indiana University Press.

Kogan, S. M., & Gale, J. E. (1997). Decentering therapy: textual analysis of a narrative session. *Family Process, 36*: 101–126.

Kohut, H. (1971). *The Analysis of the Self*. New York: International Universities Press.

Krause, I.-B. (1988). Caste and agrarian relations in North West Nepal. *Ethnos* (1–2): 5–36.

Krause, I.-B. (1989). The sinking heart: a Punjabi communication of distress. *Social Science and Medicine, 29*: 563–575.

Krause, I.-B. (1993). Anthropology and family therapy: a case for emotions. *Journal of Family Therapy, 15* (1): 35–56.

Krause, I.-B. (1994). Relationship thinking: a paradigm for medical anthropology. *British Medical Anthropology Review*, 2: 7–14.

Krause, I.-B. (1998). *Therapy across Culture.* London: Sage.

Kuper, A. (1999). *Culture: The Anthropologist's Account.* Cambridge, MA: Harvard University Press.

Kurtz, S. (1992). *All the Mothers Are One: Hindu India and the Cultural Reshaping of Psychoanalysis.* New York: Columbia University Press.

Laderman, C., & Roseman, M. (Eds.) (1996). *The Performance of Healing.* New York & London: Routledge.

Laird, J. (1998). Theorizing culture: narrative ideas and practice principles. In: M. McGoldrick (Ed.), *Revisioning Family Therapy: Race, Culture and Gender in Clinical Practice.* New York & London: Guilford Press.

Lancy, D. (1996). *Playing on the Motherground: Cultural Routines for Children's Development.* New York & London: Guilford Press.

LeVine, R. A., Dixon, S., LeVine, S., Richmen, A., Leiderman, P. H., Keefer, C. H., & Brazelton, T. B. (1994). *Childcare and Culture: Lessons from Africa.* Cambridge: Cambridge University Press.

Lewis, G. (1980). *Day of Shining Red: An Essay on Understanding Ritual.* Cambridge: Cambridge University Press.

Littlewood, R. (1991). Against pathology: the new psychiatry and its critics. *British Journal of Psychiatry, 159*: 696–702.

Littlewood, R. (1998). *The Butterfly and the Serpent: Essays in Psychiatry, Race and Religion.* London & New York: Free Association Books.

MacIntyre, A. (1970). The idea of a social science. In: B. Wilson (Ed.), *Rationality.* Oxford: Blackwell.

Macpherson, Sir William (1999). *The Stephen Lawrence Inquiry.* London: HMSO.

Main, M., & Goldwyn, R. (1984). "Adult Attachment Scoring and Classification System." Unpublished manuscript, Department of Psychology, University of California, Berkeley.

Main, M., & Goldwyn, R. (1985/1991). "Adult Attachment Scoring and

Classification System." Unpublished manuscript, Department of Psychology, University of California, Berkeley.

Malik, R. (1997). "Depression Kills More than a Self: Concepts of Mental Distress amongst Pakistanis." Unpublished PhD thesis, University of London.

Mattingly, C. (1998). *Healing Dramas and Clinical Plots: The Narrative Structure of Experience.* Cambridge: Cambridge University Press.

Maturana, H., & Varela, F. J. (1980). *Autopoiesis and Cognition: The Realization of Living.* Boston, MA: D. Reidel.

Mehta, D. (1997). *Work, Ritual, Biography: A Muslim Community in North India.* Delhi: Oxford University Press.

Minuchin, S. (1998). Where is the family in narrative family therapy? *Journal of Marital and Family Therapy, 24*: 397–403.

Minuchin, S. (1999). Retelling, reimagining and re-searching: a continuing conversation. *Journal of Marital and Family Therapy, 25* (1): 9–14.

Minuchin, S., & Fishman, H. C. (1981). *Family Therapy Techniques.* Cambridge, MA: Harvard University Press.

Nadel, S. F. (1952). Witchcraft in four African societies: an essay in comparison. *American Anthropologist, 54*: 18–29.

Nagel, T. (1986). *The View from Nowhere.* Oxford: Oxford University Press.

Nuckolls, C. W. (1998). *Culture: A Problem That Cannot Be Solved.* Madison, WI: University of Wisconsin Press.

Obeyesekere, G. (1990). *The Work of Culture: Symbolic Transformation in Psychoanalysis and Anthropology.* Chicago, IL: Chicago University Press.

Östör, A., Fruzetti, L., & Barnett, S. (1982). *Concepts of Person: Kinship, Caste and Marriage in India.* Delhi: Oxford University Press.

Parry, J. P. (1979). *Caste and Kinship in Kangra.* London & Boston, MA: Routledge & Kegan Paul.

Pocock, D. (1995). Searching for a better story: harnessing modern and postmodern positions in family therapy. *Journal of Family Therapy, 17* (2): 149–174.

Pocock, D. (1999). Therapist reflections—loose ends. *Journal of Family Therapy, 21* (2): 187–194.

*Race Relations (Amendment) Act* (2000). London: Home Office Communication Directorate.

Raffin, C., & Prata, G. (1998). From methodological to ethical rigour. *Human Systems, 9* (3–4): 203–212.

Raheja, G. G., & Gold, A. G. (1994). *Listen to the Heron's Words: Reimagining Gender and Kinship in North India.* Berkeley, CA: University of California Press.

Roland, A. (1988). *In Search of Self in India and Japan: Toward a Cross-Cultural Psychology.* Princeton, NJ: Princeton University Press.

Scarman, Lord (1981). *The Brixton Disorders, 10–12 April 1981.* Cmnd 8427. London: HMSO.

Schieffelin, E. L. (1996). On failure and performance: throwing the medium out of the seance. In: C. Laderman & M. Roseman (Eds.), *The Performance of Healing.* New York: Routledge.

Segal, L. (2000). *Why Feminism: Gender, Psychology, Politics.* Oxford: Polity Press.

Selvini Palazzoli, M., Boscolo, L., Cecchin, G., & Prata, G. (1980). *Paradox and Counter-Paradox: A New Model in the Therapy of the Family in Schizophrenic Transactions.* New York: Jason Aronson.

Shweder, R. A. (1984). Anthropology's romantic rebellion against the Enlightenment, or There's more to thinking than reason and evidence. In: R. A. Shweder & R. A. LeVine (Eds.), *Culture Theory: Essays on Mind, Self, and Emotion.* Cambridge: Cambridge University Press.

Shweder, R. A., & Bourne, E. J. (1982). Does the concept of the person vary cross-culturally. In: A. J. Marsella & G. M. White (Eds.), *Cultural Conceptions of Mental Health and Therapy.* Dordrecht: D. Reidel.

Shweder, R. A., Much, N. C., Mahapatra, M., & Park, L (1997). The "Big Three" of morality (autonomy, community, divinity) and the "Big Three" explanations of suffering. In: A. M. Brandt & P. Rozin (Eds.), *Morality and Health.* New York & London: Routledge.

Simon, R. (1992). *One to One: Conversations with Shapers of Family Therapy.* New York: Guilford Press.

Simpson, B. (1998). *Changing Families: An Ethnographic Approach to Divorce and Separation.* Oxford: Berg.

Singh, T. (1955). *English-Panjabi Dictionary.* Ludhiana: Lahore Bookshop.

Sluzki, C. E., & Ranson, D. C. (1976). *Double Bind: The Foundations of the Communicational Approach to the Family.* New York: Grune & Stratton.

Smith, B. Herrnstein, (1997). *Belief & Resistance: Dynamics of Contemporary Intellectual Controversy.* Cambridge, MA: Harvard University Press.

Strathern, M. (1999). *Property, Substance and Effect: Anthropological Essays on Persons and Things.* London: Athlone Press.

Strawson, M. (1996). In deepest sympathy: towards a natural history of virtue. Review of M. Ridley, *The Origins of Virtue. Times Literary Supplement,* 29 November, pp. 3–4.

Tamasese, K., Tuhaka, F., & Waldergrave, C. (2000). Untitled. Address delivered at conference on Institutionalised Racism and Social Justice: Therapeutic and Organisational Strategies, Institute of Family Therapy, London (2 June).

Taylor, C. (1985). *Philosophy and the Human Sciences: Philosophical Papers, 2.* Cambridge: Cambridge University Press.

Trawick, M. (1992). *Notes on Love in a Tamil Family.* Berkeley, CA: University of California Press.

Waldergrave, C. (2000). Untitled. Address delivered at conference on Institutionalised Racism and Social Justice: Therapeutic and Organisational Strategies, Institute of Family Therapy, London (2 June).

Wallerstein, I. (2000). The albatross of racism: Europe's oldest disgrace. *London Review of Books,* 18 May, pp. 11–14.

Watzlawick, P., Beavin, J., & Jackson, D. D. (1967). *Pragmatics of Human Communication.* New York: W. W. Norton.

Weingarten, K. (1998). The small and the ordinary: the daily practice of a postmodern narrative therapy. *Family Process, 37*: 3–15.

White, M. (1989). *Selected Papers.* Adelaide: Dulwich Centre Publications.

White, M. (1992). Deconstruction and therapy. In: *Experience, Contradiction, Narrative and Imagination: Selected Papers of David Epston and Michael White.* Adelaide: Dulwich Centre Publications.

White, M. (1997). *Narratives of Therapists' Lives.* Adelaide: Dulwich Centre Publications.

White, M. (2000). Exploring notions of spirituality and religion. *Context, 48* (April): 5–8.

White, M., & Epston, D. (1990). *Narrative Means to Therapeutic Ends.* New York & London: W. W. Norton.

Whyte, S. Reynolds (1997). *Questioning Misfortune: The Pragmatics of*

*Uncertainty in Eastern Uganda*. Cambridge: Cambridge University Press.

Winch, P. (1970). Understanding a primitive society. In: B. Wilson (Ed.), *Rationality*. Oxford: Blackwell.

Young, A. (1995). *The Harmony of Illusions: Inventing Post-Traumatic Stress Disorder*. Princeton, NJ: Princeton University Press.

Zimmerman, F. (1987). *The Jungle and the Aroma of Meats: An Ecological Theme in Hindu Medicine*. Berkeley, CA: University of California Press.

# INDEX